Jeannie Henderson

Reassessing ASEAN

Adelphi Paper 328

Oxford University Press, Great Clarendon Street, Oxford OX2 6DP
Oxford New York
Athens Auckland Bangkok Bombay Calcutta Cape Town
Dar es Salaam Delhi Florence Hong Kong Istanbul Karachi
Kuala Lumpur Madras Madrid Melbourne Mexico City
Nairobi Paris Singapore Taipei Tokyo Toronto
and associated companies in
Berlin Ibadan

Oxford is a trade mark of Oxford University Press

Published in the United States
by Oxford University Press Inc., New York

© The International Institute for Strategic Studies 1999

First published May 1999 by **Oxford University Press** for
The International Institute for Strategic Studies
23 Tavistock Street, London WC2E 7NQ

Director John Chipman
Editor Gerald Segal
Assistant Editor Matthew Foley
Design and Production Mark Taylor

British Library Cataloguing in Publication Data
Data available

Library of Congress Cataloguing in Publication Data

ISBN 0-19-922431-5
ISSN 0567-932x

contents

glossary

ADB	Asian Development Bank
AFTA	ASEAN Free Trade Area
APEC	Asia-Pacific Economic Cooperation forum
ARF	ASEAN Regional Forum
ASEAN	Association of South-East Asian Nations
ASEM	Asia–Europe Meeting
CGI	Consultative Group for Indonesia
CPP	Cambodian People's Party
DKBA	Democratic Karen Buddhist Army (Myanmar)
EAEC	East Asia Economic Caucus
EAEG	East Asia Economic Group
EEC	European Economic Community
EU	European Union
FPDA	Five Powers Defence Arrangements
IMF	International Monetary Fund
JIOG	Joint International Observer Group (Cambodia)
MFN	Most Favoured Nation
NAFTA	North American Free Trade Agreement
NLD	National League for Democracy (Myanmar)
NPT	Nuclear Non-Proliferation Treaty
PKI	Indonesian Communist Party
PMC	Post-Ministerial Conference

SLORC	State Law and Order Restoration Council (Myanmar)
SPDC	State Peace and Development Council (Myanmar)
TAC	Treaty of Amity and Cooperation
UNCLOS	UN Convention on the Law of the Sea
VCP	Vietnamese Communist Party
WTO	World Trade Organisation
ZOPFAN	Zone of Peace, Freedom and Neutrality

With Cambodia's admission on 30 April 1999, the Association of South-East Asian Nations (ASEAN) achieved 'the vision of the founding fathers' – the incorporation of all South-east Asian states. At the same time, the Association faced a series of unprecedented challenges stemming from its rapid enlargement, economic adversity and political transition in its most important member, Indonesia. These concerns also exposed a deeper dilemma as ASEAN sought to reconcile its central principle of non-interference in the internal affairs of its members with its goals of deeper integration, and its desire to play a more prominent role in world affairs.

Cambodia's accession capped a programme of ambitious enlargement from 1995, which also saw the entry of Vietnam, Laos and Myanmar. By contrast, only one state, Brunei in 1984, had been added to the founding five – Indonesia, Malaysia, the Philippines, Singapore and Thailand – in the 27 years since ASEAN's birth on 8 August 1967. ASEAN's rapid expansion reflected the Association's belief that it would continue to command respect, both as an economic powerhouse and as a protagonist in regional and interregional groupings.

Until July 1997, this confidence appeared well-founded. From its origins as a defensive organisation designed to reduce tensions between South-east Asia's non-communist states, ASEAN emerged from the Cold War as that region's pre-eminent institution. Despite doubts about the capacity of a child of the Cold War to adjust to new

Map 1 *ASEAN and East Asia*

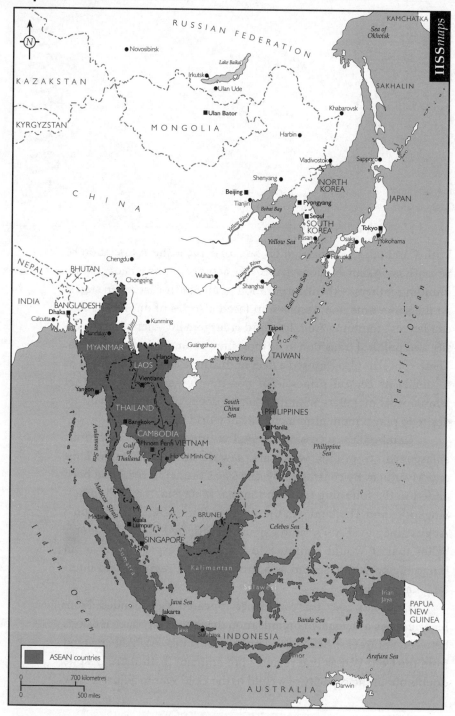

strategic circumstances, the early results were positive, even dramatic. From 1992, ASEAN established a free-trade area and embarked upon a serious attempt at market integration between its members. It expanded cooperation between South-east Asian nations to virtually all areas of public policy, promoting the idea that it had found a new path to community which would lead to an interconnectedness 'as dense as Europe's'.[1] Through the ASEAN Regional Forum (ARF), the Association initiated a multilateral security dialogue in the Asia-Pacific, which included the US, Japan, Russia and China, and established the Asia–Europe Meeting (ASEM) as a forum for discussion between Asia and Europe. For an association of predominantly small- and medium-sized developing countries, ASEAN's capacity to engage the interest and cooperation of major powers was striking. Its distinct form of regionalism – dubbed the 'ASEAN way' – became a model for other experiments in international cooperation.

However, the organisation that welcomed Cambodia in April 1999 was a pale imitation of the one which anticipated Phnom Penh's membership on its thirtieth anniversary in July 1997. Its role in managing a series of shocks – from the coup in Cambodia to the toxic smog generated by Indonesia and

many past successes were due to 'smoke and mirrors'

the collapse of the region's economies – was marginal. But this paper argues that, even before these unexpected challenges arose, ASEAN had overreached itself. The Association had no formula to reconcile its ambitious enlargement project, including the admission of the pariah state of Myanmar, with its other goals. Its apparent successes have been thrown into sharp relief, and it now seems that much of its record was obfuscated by diplomatic smoke and mirrors. Nowhere is this clearer than in the realm of economics. ASEAN had become synonymous with its members' rapid growth and economic openness, but its own programme had done little to contribute to their success, just as, when these economies failed, the Association could do little to help.

ASEAN has weathered crises before. The fall of Saigon to communist forces in 1975 and Vietnam's invasion of Cambodia in 1978 both signalled new stages in the Association's development, but did not require a fundamental change in its approach. However, enlargement, economic adversity and Indonesia's transition constitute a direct and basic challenge to the Association, and have provoked an unprecedented internal critique of the much-vaunted 'ASEAN way'.

Enlargement has significantly increased ASEAN's political and economic diversity. It has strained the Association's cohesion, revealed the limits of non-interference, complicated relations with the West and highlighted that ASEAN cannot meet international expectations when it comes to managing extreme political instability in South-east Asia. ASEAN's response to the economic crisis in key members was both late in coming, and ineffective. Its international reputation and its own self-image have been damaged, its programme of economic integration put at some risk, and trade and investment flows between new and old members disrupted. Economic and ecological problems emanating from Indonesia in the twilight of President Suharto's New Order in 1997–98 demonstrated ASEAN's limitations. While individual leaders broke with past practice and commented on the country's economic plight, within ASEAN the subject was taboo.

The internal debate within ASEAN prompted by these developments will do little to solve the fundamental contradiction between its desire to be seen as managing the region's affairs, while at the same time not interfering in the internal concerns of its members. The Association's two more liberal democracies, the Philippines and Thailand, have publicly questioned its capacity to reconcile these two objectives. This debate has resulted in the reaffirmation of the non-interference principle, accompanied by a commitment to 'enhanced interaction' – a new term in the ASEAN lexicon purportedly indicating greater frankness in discussions of cross-border issues. This formula represents little more than an uneasy truce between reform-minded members and the Association's conservative states. Keeping to it will relegate ASEAN to a marginal role in managing the new challenges facing South-east Asia.

ASEAN's setbacks also have implications beyond South-east Asia itself. The strains on the Association and its greater preoccupation with exclusively sub-regional issues limit the contribution that it can make to building an Asia-Pacific community.

ASEAN cannot command the respect that it attracted from the major powers in the early post-Cold War years. Enlargement, which sought to enhance the Association's position *vis-à-vis* China, may have convinced Beijing that ASEAN's greater diversity of strategic views – in addition to its economic problems and lack of Indonesian leadership – has in fact weakened it. Tokyo too has lowered its expectations of ASEAN's competence. The economic crisis has reaffirmed Washington's position as an indispensable political, economic and strategic player in Asia. But perceptions of American heavy-handedness have fuelled pan-Asianist feeling, at the same time as enlargement has weakened ASEAN's Western orientation. Indonesia's approach to the US will be crucial in maintaining ASEAN's commitment to Asia-Pacific, rather than pan-Asian, institutions, just as the course of its transition will be the key to clarifying ASEAN's role within the sub-region.

The success that ASEAN enjoyed in the early post-Cold War period heightened expectations among its members of the organisation's competence, and of the depth of its community. But the compact between ASEAN members is still based on loose cooperation between its governments, and on a culture of avoiding problems. Impetus for change among some original ASEAN coun-tries is countered by the conservatism of new ones. The various political orientations of ASEAN's members are reflected to an unprecedented – and uncomfortable – degree in their approach to regional cooperation. Unless ASEAN finds a coherent response to its central dilemma, its role in managing change in the region will continue to diminish.

chapter 1

ASEAN's Record

ASEAN and the Cold War

ASEAN was formed on 8 August 1967 by Indonesia, Malaysia, the Philippines, Singapore and Thailand. Its aim was to reduce tensions between South-east Asia's non-communist states, thereby freeing their weak post-colonial governments to tackle internal communist challenges, and to address development priorities.[1] Decolonisation had left a number of territorial disputes behind. The most serious demonstration of tension was the undeclared war – the *konfrontasi* or Confrontation – waged by President Sukarno's Indonesia against the new Federation of Malaysia between 1963 and 1966. Rather than an expansionist war, the Confrontation was intended to destabilise Malaysia through limited military action, economic sanctions and propaganda. It was pursued largely for domestic political reasons, and ended with Lieutenant-General Suharto's ousting of Sukarno.

ASEAN was an attempt to institutionalise the *rapprochement* between Malaysia and Indonesia, and to create a framework to build certainty and trust into relations within South-east Asia – but its founders had no clear programme for achieving this aim. The Association's founding document, the Bangkok Declaration, claimed for the countries of South-east Asia 'a primary responsibility for strengthening the economic and social stability of the region and ensuring their peaceful and progressive national development', and stated that 'they are determined to ensure their stability and security from external interference'.[2] This statement's political intent was not reflected in ASEAN's aims and purposes, which merely called for cooperation in 'economic, social, cultural, technical, scientific and administrative fields'.

While anti-communism united the Association's members, its founders defined the organisation in more conventional regional terms. The Declaration stated that ASEAN was open to all South-east Asian states subscribing to the Association's principles and goals – essentially appeals for good neighbourliness. Burma (now Myanmar) and Cambodia were asked to join, but declined on the basis that ASEAN's perceived pro-US sympathies were incompatible with their declared neutrality. The Declaration did not define South-east Asia's geographical limits, and a membership application from Ceylon (modern-day Sri Lanka) was strongly supported by Indonesia and Malaysia. It was nonetheless ultimately turned down.

In its first decade, ASEAN played a confidence-building role, opening new channels of communication between countries whose relations had been marked by 'mutual ignorance, isolation and conflict'.[3] ASEAN's more substantive claim was to have provided an incentive for South-east Asia's non-communist states to manage their differences without resorting to armed conflict. Less than a year after ASEAN's formation, Malaysia and the Philippines suspended diplomatic relations over their respective claims to Sabah.[4] When they agreed to restore relations in the following year, both countries cited the value they placed on ASEAN. But ASEAN's founders did not create the Association as a mechanism for resolving disputes between countries. From its formation, it operated on the principle of non-interference in the internal affairs of South-east Asian countries, a position formalised in the 1976 Treaty of Amity and Cooperation (TAC). The TAC created a 'high council' for formal dispute-resolution, but this has never taken place.

The non-interference principle became a guiding tenet of ASEAN for three reasons:

- first, its members feared external support for their domestic communist insurgencies;[5]
- second, ASEAN's ethnic, religious, political and economic diversity risked irreconcilable differences between its members unless these aspects of national life were excluded from discussions; and

- third, the Association's governments were unwilling to cede their new-found sovereignty, either to a supranational body, or by allowing members to comment on each other's internal affairs.

To preserve the sovereignty of its members, ASEAN's decision-making was based on consultation and consensus; issues that could not be resolved in this way were set aside. The ASEAN Secretariat, formed in 1976, was given no supranational authority.

ASEAN's guiding principles bore the strong imprint of Indonesia. Jakarta's influence stemmed from many sources, including the country's size, its large population, which was greater than that of the other ASEAN countries combined, and the legacy of *konfrontasi*, which had intimidated its neighbours. Indonesia did not openly claim a leadership role, but rather approached ASEAN according to the Javanese concept of 'leading from behind'.[6] The country's foreign policy under Suharto's New Order was low-key and development-oriented, and sought to repair the damage done by Sukarno's adventurism by subordinating its natural dominance to the interests of the region.[7] Indonesia made ASEAN the anchor of its foreign policy.

ASEAN was 'guided from behind' by Indonesia

While ASEAN claimed responsibility for maintaining the region's stability and security free from external interference, it rejected military means to achieve this end. Instead, its approach was encapsulated in the Indonesian concept of 'regional resilience', which would stem from 'national resilience' based on political and economic development, and on national defence. Ostensibly, ASEAN avoided a defence pact on the grounds that it would be provocative to those countries, implicitly Vietnam, which would be excluded. In fact, inter-state suspicion, differing threat perceptions and the focus on internal security challenges in ASEAN's early years made such a pact impossible. All ASEAN members except Indonesia – which saw its non-aligned status as a defining element of its foreign policy – had formal defence arrangements with external powers. The Philippines and Thailand were alliance partners of the US, and Malaysia and Singapore were members of the Five Powers Defence Arrangements (FPDA) with the UK, Australia and New Zealand.

ASEAN's states were divided over the practical implications of the Bangkok Declaration's proscription against external interference in managing regional affairs. In 1970, Malaysia proposed that South-east Asia should be 'neutralised' under the guarantee of the major powers. The proposal was rejected by Indonesia because neutrality at the 'diktat' of the major powers ran contrary to its concept of regional resilience, and was met with concern by both the Philippines and Singapore since it could prejudice Washington's regional presence. The resulting compromise, the Zone of Peace, Freedom and Neutrality (ZOPFAN) of 1971, committed ASEAN's states 'to exert initially necessary efforts to secure the recognition of, and respect for, South-East Asia as a Zone of Peace, Freedom and Neutrality, free from any form or manner of interference by outside Powers' – another expression of Indonesia's 'regional resilience' concept.[8] Given the differing views of neutrality's merits, no programme of implementation for ZOPFAN was developed.

Despite ZOPFAN's rhetoric, the West welcomed ASEAN's formation, and nurtured the organisation as a means of strengthening non-communist South-east Asia. From 1974, ASEAN established a series of dialogue relationships with external players, including Australia, Japan, New Zealand, Canada, the European Economic Community (EEC) and the US. Through these relationships, the West tried to encourage regionalism and a habit of consultation in South-east Asian countries. Development assistance was channelled through ASEAN, as well as through bilateral aid programmes, as a way of promoting the organisation.

ASEAN and Indochina

The communist victories in Indochina in 1975 marked a turning-point for ASEAN. In response to the changed security environment following the end of the Vietnam War, Suharto hosted the Association's first summit in February 1976, which established the TAC. Although, as an overture to Hanoi, the Treaty was 'open for accession by other states in Southeast Asia', opinion was divided in ASEAN as to whether reunified Vietnam represented a security threat, or should, as Jakarta believed, be engaged as a bulwark against China. Indonesia had broken off diplomatic relations with Beijing in 1967 in retaliation for China's alleged involvement in

Indonesia's domestic affairs through the Indonesian Communist Party (PKI), and through its possessive attitude towards the country's ethnic-Chinese community. Divided opinion over Vietnam meant that ASEAN's efforts to engage Hanoi between the 1976 summit and the Vietnamese invasion of Cambodia (then Kampuchea) in 1978 fell short of a push to secure its membership in the Association.

The installation of a pro-Hanoi regime in Phnom Penh prompted a more coherent ASEAN response. The Association waged a concerted diplomatic campaign, including in the UN, to deny the regime legitimacy, and to impose sanctions and an aid blockade in a bid to bring Hanoi to the negotiating table. Consensus over Cambodia was not, however, automatic. As a 'front-line state', Thailand demanded that ASEAN mobilise against Vietnam, while Indonesia continued to regard Hanoi as a counterweight to China.[9] ASEAN's success in denying the regime in Phnom Penh international legitimacy was due largely to the fact that both Washington and Beijing opposed Vietnam's invasion. It was therefore in the interests of both China and the US for ASEAN to mobilise international pressure.[10]

With the Soviet Union's decision to disengage from regional conflicts in the late 1980s, Vietnam was left bereft of material and diplomatic support for its Cambodian venture.[11] Following Hanoi's announcement of its military withdrawal from Cambodia, the interested parties in the conflict, including the UN Security Council's Permanent Members, were brought together in the International Conference on Cambodia in July–August 1989, co-chaired by France and

Cambodia helps ASEAN come of age

Indonesia. Although the conference failed to find a settlement, the peace process was able to move forward. In October 1991, the Paris Peace Accords were concluded with an agreement that democratic elections would be held in Cambodia under UN auspices.

Although ASEAN played its role over Cambodia at the convenience of the US and China, the Association nonetheless emerged from the process as 'the third world's most successful experiment in regionalism', and a diplomatic player capable of intervening on a major issue of regional security.[12] This was a marked change from its first decade, when its voice was heard principally on issues such as trade and aid. On the one hand, the Association's experience over Cambodia laid the foundations for the greater diplomatic role it would seek following the end of the Cold War. On the other, however, the Paris Accords, which were fashioned between the major powers, demonstrated that ASEAN's claim to manage regional order free from external interference had not been upheld.[13]

Opportunities and Challenges after the Cold War

The Soviet Union's disintegration presented ASEAN with challenges, as well as opportunities. The Association emerged from the Cold War as South-east Asia's pre-eminent institution, in a position to contemplate enlargement on its own terms. It could boast over two decades of peace among its members, accompanied by increasingly strong economic performance. The overall security environment had dramatically improved with the disappearance of Sino-Soviet rivalry. In 1989, China had clarified its position on ethnic Chinese in South-east Asia, accepting their local citizenship and removing an important block in relations, particularly with Jakarta. By 1991, Indonesia, Singapore and Brunei had become the last ASEAN countries to normalise relations with China.

At the same time, the Cold War's end threatened ASEAN's cohesion and its diplomatic aspirations. For Singaporean Prime Minister Goh Chok Tong, the post-Cold War challenge was to 'keep ASEAN relevant and sought after in a situation where the great powers no longer need to compete for ASEAN's support and the European Community and North America are forming economic blocs'.[14] The positive developments in relations with China were accompanied by concerns over the country's growing might, which now went unchecked by the Soviet Union. Washington's announcement in November 1991 that it would withdraw from its military bases in the Philippines heightened ASEAN's apprehension. While US withdrawal was consistent with the Association's 1967 declaration on the temporary nature of foreign bases, members nonetheless sought reassurance that the base closures did not signify a decline in US strategic commitments.

ASEAN leaders held their first post-Cold War summit in Singapore in January 1992, from which a range of initiatives emerged. Leaders sought to bolster 'regional resilience' by deepening cooperation between their countries, and by laying the groundwork for the Association to absorb the remaining South-east Asian states. They indicated their increased commitment to ASEAN, and agreed that formal summits would be held every three years, rather than on an *ad hoc* basis, with the provision for informal ones in intervening years. The Association's leaders also decided that, for the first time, the annual ministerial-level meeting with dialogue partners could deal with security issues. This reflected a desire to underpin US engagement and encourage China's participation as a responsible power. Immediately after the summit, concerns about China were reinforced when it formalised its claim to the islands of the South China Sea by promulgating a law on territorial waters. China's claims put it in dispute with Brunei, Malaysia, the Philippines and Vietnam, all of which claimed parts or all of the Spratly Islands and surrounding maritime areas.

While ASEAN contemplated its new agenda, its members fully intended to keep to the founding principle of non-interference in each other's internal affairs. The Association had not commented on Indonesia's annexation of East Timor in 1976, and its members voted against UN resolutions criticising Jakarta over the territory. Only rarely had it deviated from this practice. In 1986, it issued a modest statement calling for 'a peaceful solution to the crisis' in the Philippines between President Ferdinand Marcos and pro-democracy leader Corazon Aquino.[15] Also in 1986, Malaysia strongly criticised Singapore's hosting of a state visit by then Israeli President Chaim Herzog.[16] These exceptions to the rule illustrate the defining impact that non-interference has had on the conduct of diplomacy between ASEAN's members, both multilaterally and bilaterally.

Deepening Cooperation

The 1992 Singapore summit established AFTA, initiating an economic programme that was to be the essence of the Association's attempt to deepen cooperation between its members. Throughout the 1970s and 1980s, ASEAN had intermittently and unsuccessfully tried to develop an economic agenda in line with its founding commitment to cooperation. By 1992, its members had achieved substantial unilateral liberalisation and, as increasingly aggressive exporters, were concerned that the European Union (EU) or the

Figure 1 *ASEAN Trade, 1992*

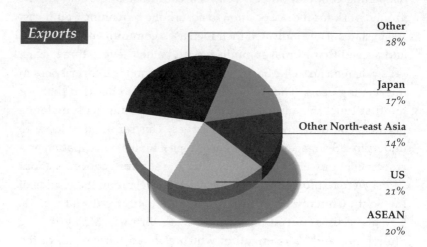

Exports

Other
28%

Japan
17%

Other North-east Asia
14%

US
21%

ASEAN
20%

North American Free Trade Agreement (NAFTA) states could become inward-looking trade blocs.

When the decision to establish AFTA was taken, trade between ASEAN's members accounted for around 20% of ASEAN's total trade. At the outset, therefore, AFTA was as much about building post-Cold War cohesion and increasing ASEAN's credibility as it was an attempt to boost the region's gross domestic product.[17] AFTA members agreed to a 15-year timetable for harmonising their tariffs at between zero and 5%. This schedule was criticised as too long, while the scheme excluded significant sectors, including unprocessed agricultural goods. Attempts to remedy these deficiencies were made in 1994, when the deadline was brought forward to 2003, and unprocessed agricultural products were included. Later agreements, known as 'AFTA plus', reinforced the commitment to more economic integration by harmonising customs and product standards. Initial agreements were also reached on trade in services, and on investment liberalisation.

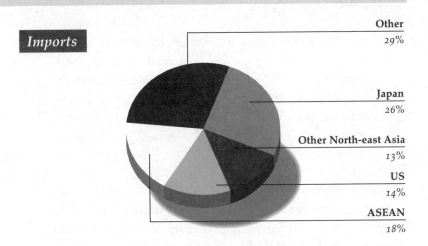

Imports

Other
29%

Japan
26%

Other North-east Asia
13%

US
14%

ASEAN
18%

Source   East Asia Analytical Unit, *ASEAN Free Trade Area: Trading Bloc or Building Block* (Canberra: Commonwealth of Australia, April 1994), pp. 66–67

Before 1992, ASEAN's economic agenda had emphasised national sovereignty, and had avoided the term 'integration' in favour of the looser concept of 'cooperation'.[18] While AFTA could never transform the region's economy given the low share of trade between ASEAN members, by the end of 1995 AFTA and 'AFTA plus' represented a plausible attempt at market integration – before it was achieved in other groupings, such as APEC, or globally through the World Trade Organisation (WTO). The legally binding nature of AFTA commitments and the role of the ASEAN Secretariat in monitoring observance of the scheme contrasted with the essentially consultative nature of much of ASEAN's functional cooperation.

This cooperation continued to expand, with 250 meetings held annually and regular ministerial contact extended beyond the foreign and trade ministries of Association members. In 1992, the ASEAN Secretariat was given additional resources, and its Secretary-General position upgraded to Secretary-General of

ASEAN, with minister-equivalent status. Singaporean scholar Chin Kin Wah has argued that:

> *ASEAN (with its enhanced secretariat, regularized summits, as well as more regular informal heads of government meetings, its varied ministerial and official level meetings, and dialogues with extra-regional states ...) can lay claim to being the most extensively institutionalized (but not supra-nationalized) regional association besides the European Union.*[19]

At its 1995 summit, ASEAN's leaders emphasised the concept of an 'ASEAN community'. Singaporean Prime Minister Goh, for example, claimed that 'over time, our region's interconnectedness will be as dense as Europe's. And we will grow closer together as a community'.[20] These aspirations to community were echoed by Fidel Ramos, at the time the president of the Philippines, who called for ASEAN to launch a 'final ascent to the heights of mutuality, integration and community'.[21] The Association's leaders also expressed the view that ASEAN should be relevant to the daily lives of South-east Asia's people, and that the region's states should forge non-governmental, as well as government-level, links.

Enlarging ASEAN

At its 1992 summit, ASEAN leaders stated that the Association would 'forge a closer relationship based on friendship and cooperation with the Indo-Chinese countries, following the settlement on Cambodia'. They also emphasised that the TAC was open for signature by all South-east Asian states. In July 1992, Vietnam and Laos signed the treaty, and attended the ASEAN Ministerial Meeting as observers. As in 1975–78, there were differences between ASEAN members over the speed of Vietnam's engagement. Singapore was wary of introducing a communist country into the Association, while Vietnam's long-time enemy, Thailand, supported *rapprochement* as a way of converting 'battlefields to market places'. Unlike the post-reunification period, Hanoi was receptive to ASEAN's overtures. The admission process moved rapidly, with Vietnam receiving a formal invitation to join in 1994. The country became ASEAN's seventh member at the Ministerial Meeting in Brunei on 28 July 1995. Vietnam's incorporation was a unique opportunity to cement the new peace in South-east Asia, increasing stability and bolstering the region *vis-à-vis* China.

The admission process for Laos, which began at the same time as Vietnam's, moved more slowly because of the country's limited diplomatic capacity. At the Brunei meeting, Laos announced its wish to join ASEAN in 1997, the Association's thirtieth anniversary year. Also in 1995, Cambodia assumed observer status. Phnom Penh's coalition government, which came to power through the UN-supervised polls in 1993, had initially seemed reluctant to participate in ASEAN, possibly reflecting King Sihanouk's continued influence (Sihanouk had kept Cambodia out of ASEAN in 1967). This position soon showed signs of movement, and Cambodia's co-prime ministers, Prince Norodom Ranariddh and Hun Sen, attended ASEAN's Bangkok summit in December 1995 – the first to include all South-east Asian states.

ASEAN also renewed attempts to incorporate Myanmar (as Burma became in 1989). Since 1967, the Association had periodically tried to encourage it to join, but Burma had held to its autarkic, isolationist and non-aligned posture.[22] ASEAN's new drive to engage Myanmar from 1990 stemmed from concern over China's increasing influence there; according to Suharto, Myanmar's admission was necessary to avoid 'ASEAN's

Myanmar's membership was supposed to help break Chinese encirclement

encirclement by China'.[23] ASEAN countries were also developing substantial business interests in Myanmar. However, the regime's bloody suppression of the pro-democracy movement in 1988, the arrest of its leader, Aung San Suu Kyi, and the annulment of the results of the 1990 election, which the regime resoundingly lost, meant that ASEAN's overtures risked damaging its relations with the West. At the same time, the West's isolation of Myanmar – depriving it of trade, investment and aid at a time when the economy was close to collapse – was behind Yangon's decision to respond to the Association.

To deal with Myanmar while responding to Western pressure, ASEAN coined the phrase 'constructive engagement', which first appeared in the South-east Asian lexicon in 1991.[24] Constructive engagement – defined by the *Straits Times* as 'gentle persuasion and quiet diplomacy to prod the regime into political liberalisation' – was premised on the idea that, by opening channels of communication and bringing foreign trade and investment into the country's closed economy, Myanmar would move towards political reform.[25] ASEAN's approach was, however, tentative, reflecting the discomfort that stemmed from the tension between constructive engagement and the principle of non-interference. The Association initially set 2000 as the target date for Myanmar's admission, and the country attended the ASEAN Ministerial Meetings in 1994 and 1995 as a guest of the host governments, rather than as an observer. Despite opposition to Myanmar's admission from the US and the EU, the timetable was accelerated in 1996 when Myanmar was given observer status, reflecting the Association's determination to manage South-east Asian affairs, and to stand up to pressure from the major powers.[26] In the following year, both Myanmar and Laos were admitted to ASEAN.

Beyond South-East Asia

Although multilateral defence cooperation had been excluded from ASEAN's agenda in its first two decades, common membership and the experience of dialogue and confidence-building allowed bilateral military cooperation between ASEAN members to flourish by the early 1990s.[27] This 'defence spiderweb' did not, however, constitute the basis for establishing an ASEAN defence community. Different threat perceptions, notably over China, and lingering suspicions between some ASEAN states meant that the Association continued to use non-military means to promote its security.[28]

At its 1992 summit, ASEAN leaders indicated that the Association should 'intensify its external dialogues in political and security matters using the ASEAN Post-Ministerial Conferences'. Singapore assumed the key role, developing this broad directive into a proposal for a regional security dialogue encompassing the whole of the Asia-Pacific.[29] Australia and Canada had proposed such a dialogue in 1990, as had Japan in 1991. The formative meeting of the ARF, a foreign-minister-level security forum involving ASEAN, its dialogue partners, China, Russia, Vietnam, Laos and Papua New

Guinea, took place in 1993. Its first working session was held the following year. The ARF was a recognition that any separation of South-east Asia's security from that of the North-east was artificial. Suspicion among the major powers meant that ASEAN was able to claim the position as the ARF's 'prime driving force'. It was also acknowledged as the model from which the Forum derived its principles of consultation and consensus, its emphasis on commonality and its minimal institutionalisation.

The creation of the APEC forum in 1989 had given impetus to the idea of a regional security dialogue. APEC was proposed by Australia, which pursued it jointly with South Korea. The forum, which was initially a dialogue between the 18 Asia-Pacific economies, adopted in 1994 the specific goal of regional free trade and investment by 2010 for developed countries, and by 2020 for developing ones. ASEAN's role in APEC differed from the one that it played in the ARF. ASEAN countries had responded to the Australian initiative individually, and had attended APEC's first ministerial meeting before the Association had produced a 'common position' on its participation.[30] The forum is not exclusively chaired by Association members. Although ASEAN forms a caucus within APEC, the diversity in levels of economic development between Association countries has meant that the interests of individual states – particularly Singapore – are often more closely aligned with non-ASEAN members, leading them to band together. Nonetheless, ASEAN 'solidarity' has had an impact on APEC's development. It is unclear, for example, whether the forum's free-trade targets would have been achieved without the influence which their progenitor, Suharto, brought to bear on his ASEAN colleagues. On the other hand, individual countries have invoked ASEAN solidarity to defeat liberalisation proposals, particularly in investment.

APEC and the ARF emerged as complementary processes giving structure to the post-Cold War Asia-Pacific. While the US had been sceptical of earlier proposals for multilateral security arrangements in the region, the ARF was well received by President Bill Clinton's newly elected administration, which saw its backing for both the ARF and APEC in terms of an emerging 'Pacific community'. Japan regarded the ARF's multilateral security dialogue as an opportunity to expand its security role in a nonthreatening way, consistent with its pacifist constitution. ASEAN's claim to stewardship of the process was, however, only reluctantly accepted.

ASEAN's central aim in establishing the ARF was to bring China into structures that would encourage it to play a responsible role in the region. Beijing's South China Sea claims (see Map 2, page 59) were the greatest cause for concern. In response to their formalisation in 1992, ASEAN had issued the Manila Declaration on the South China Sea, which called for all issues of sovereignty and jurisdiction to be resolved peacefully. The Association's worst fears were realised in February 1995, when Manila revealed that China had seized Mischief Reef, a rocky outcrop within the Philippines' Exclusive Economic Zone. In the following April, ASEAN confronted Beijing over Mischief Reef, and did so again three months later in the ARF.

> ## ASEAN wanted the ARF to help 'civilise' China

ASEAN's unexpected resistance over Mischief Reef coincided with continuing efforts to build an institutional relationship with China. This process had begun in 1991, when then Chinese Foreign Minister Qian Qichen attended the opening ceremony of the ASEAN Ministerial Meeting in Kuala Lumpur as a guest of the Malaysian government. It ended in July 1996, when China became one of ASEAN's dialogue partners. Beijing's responsiveness to ASEAN contained an element of competition with Washington, requiring the Association to juggle its aim to improve relations with China with the need to avoid undermining US strategic engagement. It thus tried to position itself as an interlocutor between Washington and Beijing, a stance made most explicit in the ARF, where the Association emphasised its unique ability to bring the major powers together.

Beneath the institutional consensus on the US presence in Asia, ASEAN's members placed differing emphasis on the importance of consolidating US engagement, as opposed to maintaining the Association's manoeuvrability. As East Asia's 'economic miracle' was popularised, and ASEAN countries recorded some of the world's highest growth-rates, Malaysia continued to promote an East Asia Economic Group (EAEG). Kuala Lumpur had initially proposed this structure, which would have excluded the US, Australia and New Zealand, the year after APEC was formed. It was opposed by the US and by Japan, which was concerned that it would divide the Pacific, both economically and strategically. A recast proposal – dubbed the East Asia Economic Caucus (EAEC) – was nominally endorsed by ASEAN as a caucus within APEC in July 1992, but has never functioned as such.

Growing economic confidence coincided with claims by some South-east Asian leaders – most prominently Singapore's elder statesman Lee Kuan Yew and Malaysian Prime Minister Mahathir Mohamad – and commentators that there was a unique set of 'Asian values'.[31] These included deference to society over the individual, thrift, respect for authority, and attachment to the family. At the height of these intellectual trends, ASEAN considered a Singaporean proposal for East Asian summitry based around its own meetings. In 1995, leaders agreed that informal summits could include countries other than ASEAN states, but differences within the Association meant that the composition of the non-member invitees was left to the discretion of the summit host. Indonesia, host of the first informal summit in 1996, confined them to Cambodia, Laos and Myanmar.

ASEAN's success in establishing the ARF made the Association increasingly confident in seeking a global role. In 1994, Singapore proposed setting up a meeting of Asian and European states, and, the following year, the idea received the backing of its ASEAN partners. Europe's response was also positive, possibly because of its perception that it had failed to engage with the world's fastest-growing region; certainly, the economic success of the ASEAN states boosted the Association's diplomatic credibility.[32] ASEM, which held its inaugural summit in March 1996, was presented as the third side of the US–Europe–Asia triangle, and covered political, economic and strategic issues. ASEAN's role in ASEM fell between its formal position as the ARF's 'driving force', and its minimal institutional presence in APEC. It has nonetheless steered the Asian side of the ASEM process.[33]

ASEAN's conclusion of the South-East Asian Nuclear Weapons Free Zone treaty in 1995, without the agreement of the nuclear powers to the protocol to which they were expected to adhere, was a further indication of the Association's early post-Cold War confidence. Since all South-east Asian states had signed the Nuclear Non-Proliferation Treaty (NPT), the regional treaty would affect only the declared nuclear-weapon powers. Negotiations for the treaty had begun in 1984, but were strongly opposed by the US, raising concerns in the Philippines, Singapore and Thailand. In the more benign post-Cold War environment, ASEAN revisited the concept, accelerated negotiations and signed the treaty in Bangkok in December 1995.

Successes and Dilemmas

While the major powers recognised that ASEAN's regionalism was not that of the EU, the Association nonetheless often managed to speak with one voice, and was encouraged to do so by the US, the EU and Japan. For Europe, the opportunity to deal with a group of predominantly small and medium-sized nations as a single unit was attractive given its attempts to forge a corporate foreign-policy identity. ASEAN's success in engaging Europe was largely the result of its reputation as an economic powerhouse – to which its pro-gramme of economic cooperation through AFTA had actually contributed little. The US, while maintaining a bilateral approach to South-east Asia, found it useful to regard ASEAN as a single player in its Asia-Pacific plans. In 1995, then US Secretary of State Warren Christopher noted that the US 'is committed to working with ASEAN in a full and equal partnership that covers a broad range of shared security, economic and political interests'.[34] These expectations encouraged the international community to turn to ASEAN to respond to Co-Prime Minister Hun Sen's coup in Cambodia in July 1997. But this offer of a leadership role for ASEAN overlooked the extent to which the part that the Association had played over Cambodia in the 1980s, and in the Paris Peace Accords, had been at the convenience of the major powers.

Likewise, ASEAN's expansion and its attempts to deepen cooperation between its members created problems and dilemmas. Achieving ASEAN-10 comprising all South-east Asian states would, it was claimed, raise the Association's diplomatic profile. At ASEAN's 1995 summit, Ramos declared that 'progress toward a Southeast Asian community would add considerable weight to

ASEAN – in its influence in the world and in dealing with the big powers'.[35] This view was echoed by Mahathir: 'The political and economic potentials which ASEAN would have, as an enlarged grouping, to determine ASEAN's own destiny, and to influence the pace and direction of Asia Pacific affairs, is really quite enormous'.[36] But enlargement ignored the complications of Myanmar's pariah status in the majority of Western capitals. In terms of the claims to deeper integration, much of the Association's functional cooperation amounted to networking and information-sharing, rather than real efforts to standardise public policy. Even before the unprecedented challenges that beset ASEAN as it entered the final stage of enlargement, the expectations surrounding ASEAN-10 were inflated.

ASEAN's Challenges

chapter 2

Between 1992 and its thirtieth anniversary in July 1997, ASEAN widened and deepened, and played an active role in the Asia-Pacific and beyond. It took advantage of post-Cold War fluidity and the difficult relations between the region's major powers to establish a leading role in the ARF, and built on this success to begin a dialogue with Europe. Since its anniversary, however, ASEAN has lurched from crisis to crisis, and has had only a marginal impact on Southeast Asian affairs. This reversal of fortune is the result of three coincident challenges: enlargement, economic adversity and Indonesia's political transition following the resignation of Suharto in May 1998. These developments prompted some ASEAN members to question the Association's ability to act as a regional manager, while at the same time keeping to its traditional working methods. Unless ASEAN finds a response to its crises to which all its members can agree, its role in managing change in the region will continue to decline.

Enlargement

ASEAN's enlargement promised to extend to the whole of Southeast Asia the peaceful and prosperous culture of cooperation established by the Association's original members. In signing the TAC, Vietnam, Laos, Myanmar and Cambodia committed themselves to preventing disputes from arising with their neighbours, and renounced the threat or use of force to resolve disagreements.

ASEAN's vast range of cooperative activities would open channels of communication between countries, benefit bilateral relations and emphasise shared interests. But enlargement's expectations went beyond the original vision of achieving cooperation between former adversaries. It was intended to increase ASEAN's diplomatic standing by allowing it to speak for the whole of South-east Asia.[1] It was also designed to bolster the Association's standing in relation to China by incorporating the strategically significant and populous Vietnam, and by reducing Beijing's influence in Myanmar.

Enlargement would also be costly. Although ASEAN prided itself on its 'unity in diversity', enlargement substantially increased its political and economic variety, and the diversity of strategic views among its members. The Association's political spectrum broadened with the inclusion of the communist governments of Vietnam and Laos, and of Myanmar's authoritarian military regime, just as liberal democracy was becoming more entrenched in the Philippines and Thailand. With Myanmar's 'constructive engagement', through which original members exerted subtle pressure on Yangon to reform, the Association acknowledged that the political profile of its new members could not be ignored. Economically, the new membership extended the range of per-capita gross national product from Singapore's \$32,940 to Cambodia's \$300, and Vietnam's \$320.[2] Singapore, with one of the world's most open economies, now rubbed shoulders with countries retaining elements of central planning. The limited institutional capacity of the new entrants, an important consideration given that the Association's chairing responsibilities rotated between members, risked further strain on ASEAN's cohesion. Given their past international isolation, it was likely that the newcomers would feel uncomfortable with ASEAN's familial atmosphere, and with its practice of consensus-building and compromise.

Vietnam

Vietnam's admission into ASEAN in 1995 has been described as 'a historic act of reconciliation'.[3] Its symbolism was enormous. ASEAN had been created as a bulwark against communism, the ideology to which Vietnam continued to subscribe, albeit in a modified form. During the Cold War, Hanoi had viewed the Association as a 'tool' of

Table I *ASEAN's Diversity*

	Population ('000)	Total Area (km²)	GDP (1998 US$bn)
Brunei	317	5,770	4.9
Cambodia	10,430	181,040	2.9
Indonesia	200,745	1,919,440	88.6
Laos	5,200	236,800	1.1
Malaysia	22,000	329,750	67.5
Myanmar	49,500	678,500	19.0
Philippines	74,044	300,000	64.5
Singapore	3,076	648	84.4
Thailand	62,910	514,000	117.0
Vietnam	78,852	329,560	24.6

Note   GDP figures for Brunei, Cambodia and Myanmar are estimated

Sources *The Military Balance, 1998/99* (Oxford: Oxford University Press for the
         IISS, 1998); *World Factbook 1998* (Washington DC: Directorate of
         Intelligence, 1998); International Monetary Fund; US State Department,
         www.state.gov; Australian Department of Foreign Affairs and Trade,
         www.dfat.gov.au

the US.[4] The end of the Cold War and Vietnam's withdrawal from Cambodia redefined relations between ASEAN and Vietnam. Hanoi's admission could help to heal the Indochina divide by opening channels of communication and providing incentives to manage and resolve disputes. Relations between Thailand and Vietnam, whose enmity predated the Cold War and was played out in pre-colonial times through competition for influence in Cambodia, is a testing-ground for this process. Officials in Hanoi argue that ASEAN membership has provided additional impetus to resolve a number of long-standing differences.[5] In August 1997, both countries concluded an agreement on sea boundaries, and they have also reached agreement on disputed fisheries. Under the 1991 Paris Peace Accords, Thailand and Vietnam, together with the other signatories, committed themselves not to interfere in Cambodia's internal affairs. As signatories to the TAC, both are also bound by the principle of non-interference in South-east Asia's states, including Cambodia. As the Paris Accords age, the TAC and shared member-ship of ASEAN reinforce the commitment which Thailand and Vietnam made in 1991.

Vietnam has made great efforts to adapt to ASEAN's consensual and familial atmosphere. It joined the emerging Asso-ciation consensus to postpone Cambodia's admission following Hun Sen's coup in July 1997, despite important reasons to argue for Phnom Penh's entry to take place on schedule. Hun Sen's govern-ment grew out of the regime installed by Vietnam 18 years earlier, and conservatives within the Vietnamese Communist Party (VCP) were reluctant to damage this relationship. The Vietnamese government was also concerned that the break with the principle of non-interference implied by the postponement could set a precedent for ASEAN to take account of a country's political situation in its decision-making.

Hanoi has invested heavily in attending ASEAN meetings, establishing an ASEAN infrastructure within its bureaucracy and hosting the Association's sixth summit in December 1998. In this, Hanoi has been helped by the generally high quality of its foreign service, and by its officials' facility in English, ASEAN's lingua franca. Other ASEAN capitals regard Hanoi's efforts to adapt to the Association's informal and consensus-based style as remarkable, given the country's communist system and its recent isolation. As one ASEAN official put it in 1998, it was easy to forget that Vietnam was a new member.[6]

Vietnam's admission into ASEAN coincided with the normal-isation of relations with the US, and with its acceptance into ASEM and then APEC. ASEAN's approach to Vietnam chimed with the West's desire to see Hanoi join the international and regional main-stream. There has been no tension between ASEAN's incorporation of Vietnam, and its pursuit of a greater role in global affairs.

Myanmar

ASEAN has not achieved the goals that it set for Myanmar's incorporation in 1997. It was hoped that participating in ASEAN would ease Myanmar away from its isolationist mindset and could, over time, encourage greater openness in its society. Through its membership, Myanmar is exposed to over 250 meetings a year, including at head-of-government and ministerial levels. However, the country has been a relatively silent partner in ASEAN's major fora. Although anecdotal evidence suggests that officials participate actively in the ASEAN process in technical and administrative areas, the majority of those involved are civilians with little influence in Yangon.[7] Myanmar's ability to participate in the Association's web of economic, social and cultural cooperation is severely circumscribed by the abnormal conditions prevailing within the country. Myanmar's involvement in the ASEAN University Network, for example, is meaningless because all major universities have been closed since 1995.

For some ASEAN states, primarily Indonesia, Myanmar's membership was intended to limit China's strategic influence in South-east Asia. But the Association's ability to compete with China for influence in the country was limited even before the crisis of July 1997. ASEAN could offer Yangon a degree of international credibility, but also would need to match the more immediate benefits of its relationship with China, namely economic support and arms sales. The Association cannot, however, compete with China in providing military assistance, while economic adversity has made it more difficult for ASEAN to offer Myanmar trade and investment benefits.

Myanmar is also a source of various security threats, including refugee flows, cross-border incursions, drug production and AIDS. It was hoped that membership would provide an incentive for the regime to manage these issues. Yangon does not, however, seem prepared to follow ASEAN's rules of self-restraint in relations with its neighbours. Six months after its admission, a spate of incursions by the Democratic Karen Buddhist Army (DKBA), an ethnic splinter group aligned with the Yangon regime, led to the death of a number of refugees in Thailand. Bangkok was criticised for its failure to protect refugee camps, and, although Thai Prime Minister Chuan Leekpai publicly accepted the regime's claim that the raiders were beyond its control, it is likely that they had its tacit support.[8]

The regime has also failed to offer sustained political concessions in response to ASEAN's 'constructive engagement'. In private meetings with their Myanmar counterparts, ASEAN leaders have advised on political issues, and have encouraged the regime to open a dialogue with the pro-democracy opposition.[9] The foreign ministers of the Philippines and Malaysia met pro-democracy leader Aung San Suu Kyi in October 1997 and March 1998 respectively. In June 1997, Malaysian Foreign Minister Abdullah Badawi, acting as ASEAN's envoy, also tried to persuade the regime to establish a dialogue. Since the approaches of individual governments differ, there is agreement that constructive engagement must be a bilateral process (Badawi's 1997 visit was an exception), and that approaches should be private and high-level. Yangon has tolerated the majority of these representations as the price for ASEAN membership, while limiting the domestic impact of the Association's implicit criticism through its control of the media. The private nature of the representations by ASEAN leaders has made this task easier, while the regime denied that the meeting between Aung San Suu Kyi and Philippines Foreign Minister Domingo Siazon had taken place.

There is little sign that constructive engagement has modified Yangon's behaviour. The regime has made some concessions, such as allowing visits by Alvaro de Soto, special envoy of UN Secretary-General Kofi Annan, to resume after a two-year hiatus, but the slight political opening and more substantial economic reforms of 1995 have been reversed. Although Yangon portrayed the transition from the State Law and Order Restoration Council (SLORC) to the State Peace and Development Council (SPDC) in November 1997 as the 'emergence of a new generation of leaders', it is not clear that the SPDC is any more reformist than its predecessor.[10] On the eve of the ASEAN meetings in July 1998, the military government arrested a number of opposition figures and issued a thinly veiled threat that pressure for reform would be met with violence. The National League for Democracy (NLD)'s network has been systematically undermined since the SPDC's formation, while economic deterioration has accelerated. Foreign investment has dried up, reflecting lack of confidence in the reform programme and economic contraction in ASEAN countries.

Cambodia

Cambodia became ASEAN's tenth member on 30 April 1999, almost two years after its intended admission date. Under ASEAN's non-interference principle, Hun Sen's 1997 coup should not have affected the timetable for the country's admission. However, ASEAN had several pressing reasons to ignore its principle and postpone Cambodia's entry:

- first, Suharto, ASEAN's elder statesman, was intent on punishing Hun Sen for his disregard for the Association's image;
- second, the international community looked to ASEAN to lead the diplomatic response to the coup, a role which it could not have played had it kept to its non-interference principle; and
- third, ASEAN was concerned that admitting Myanmar and Cambodia at the same time would have damaged its reputation in the West.

Even so, the non-interference issue was divisive: conservative members accepted the postponement and subsequent ASEAN mediation as a pragmatic response to international expectations in an exceptional set of circumstances, rather than as setting a precedent.

Having postponed Cambodia's membership, ASEAN was compelled to outline the political conditions under which the country would be admitted – a return to coalition government and free and fair elections. At the urging of the international community, the Association unwillingly mediated between the Cambodian parties through a troika comprising the foreign ministers of Indonesia, the Philippines and Thailand. This was a role for which it was unprepared, and with which it was uncomfortable. Sensing the Association's vulnerability, Hun Sen explicitly rejected the ASEAN troika, and accused the Association of violating its own central principle. As international pressure mounted, he accepted the troika – but with the proviso that it did not interfere in Cambodia's internal affairs. By early 1998, the troika had made almost no progress, and Japan intervened with its 'Four Pillars' proposal, covering a ceasefire, the return of political exiles, severing links between ousted royalists and the illegal Khmer Rouge, and free and fair elections. Tokyo's position as Cambodia's major aid donor was important in securing Hun Sen's acceptance of its initiative, laying the basis for elections on 26 July 1998. A UN-coordinated Joint International Observer Group (JIOG) declared the polls credible, as did ASEAN. Hun Sen's Cambodian People's Party (CPP) won the largest number of seats in the legislature but, because it fell short of the two-thirds majority needed to form a government in its own right, entered into a coalition with Ranariddh's royalists.

Further instability in Cambodia could again prompt differences between ASEAN members over the Association's appropriate role. Phnom Penh's troubled admission demonstrates the limits to ASEAN's approach to regional management, and highlights that the Association cannot meet the expectations of the international community when it comes to tackling extreme political instability in South-east Asia.

Like Cambodia, Laos is one of South-east Asia's smallest and poorest countries, and has great difficulty in meeting its ASEAN obligations.[11] This has implications for ASEAN's pursuit of deeper integration, and for its performance as a diplomatic player. Vientiane's lack of bureaucratic capacity is likely to take its toll when Laos is required to chair the Association, or to assume responsibility for areas of international cooperation.

Economic Adversity

With the exception of the Philippines, all the original ASEAN states enjoyed high economic growth throughout the 1970s and 1980s. Between 1991 and 1996, this growth became spectacular, and the Association's economies became key parts of the so-called 'East Asian economic miracle'. Thailand averaged 7.9% growth, Malaysia 8.7%, Indonesia 7.8% and Singapore 8.5%. Even the economy of the Philippines – often described as 'the sick man of Asia' – grew by 5.9% in 1996.

With the Thai baht's devaluation in mid-1997, catastrophe struck. The baht was floated on 2 July in response to capital flight, which had made defending the currency cripplingly costly. It immediately fell by 12%; within three weeks, the Malaysian ringgitt,

Table 2 *GDP Growth in ASEAN States, 1991–1998*

(%)	1991	1992	1993	1994	1995	1996	1997	1998
Brunei	4.0	-1.1	0.5	1.8	3.0	3.5	–	–
Cambodia	7.6	7.0	4.1	4.0	7.6	7.0	1.0	0
Indonesia	8.9	7.2	7.3	7.5	8.2	8.0	4.7	-13.7
Laos	4.0	7.0	5.9	8.2	7.1	6.9	6.5	5.0
Malaysia	8.6	7.8	8.4	9.3	9.4	8.6	7.7	-6.8
Myanmar	-0.7	9.7	5.9	6.8	7.2	6.4	4.0	1.1
Philippines	-0.6	0.3	2.1	4.4	4.7	5.9	5.2	-0.5
Singapore	7.3	6.2	10.4	10.5	8.9	7.5	8.0	1.5
Thailand	8.1	8.2	8.5	8.6	8.8	5.5	-0.4	-8.0
Vietnam	6.0	8.7	8.1	8.8	9.5	9.3	8.8	3.5

Note   Figures for 1996, 1997 and 1998 for Myanmar are estimated

Sources   International Monetary Fund; US State Department, www.state.gov;
          Australian Department of Foreign Affairs and Trade, www.dfat.gov.au;
          ASEAN Secretariat, www.aseansec.org

Indonesian rupiah and Philippine peso had also slumped. In August, the Thai government negotiated a $17 billion rescue package with the International Monetary Fund (IMF). In Indonesia, broadening the band in which the rupiah could move caused it to fall heavily and, on 8 October, Jakarta announced that it too would seek IMF help. A $23bn package was unveiled on 31 October, and assistance eventually totalled $43bn. A series of economic measures announced by the Malaysian government was described as the 'IMF without the IMF'.

The economic crisis forced the resignation of Thai Prime Minister Chavalit Yongchaiyudh on 6 November, and a new government with strong reformist credentials was formed. In Indonesia, difficulties in implementing the first IMF agreement led to a second, signed by Suharto and IMF Managing Director Michel Camdessus on 15 January 1998. However, market uncertainty over whether Jakarta was actually prepared to implement the new agreement drove the rupiah below 17,000 to the US dollar, from a level of 2,500 before the crisis. Dissatisfied with the IMF's prescriptions, the Indonesian government explored alternatives, including a currency board, which led the Fund to threaten to terminate its rescue plan. Economic turmoil prompted rioting across the country. Suharto's absence at a G-15 summit of developing nations in Cairo in May 1998 provided the catalyst for students to mobilise peacefully against the government in Jakarta and other cities. After the shooting by security forces of four student demonstrators at Jakarta's Trisakti University, mobs rampaged through the capital, burning and looting; some 1,200 people died. Suharto, having lost the crucial support of the army, resigned on 20 May. The new government, headed by former Vice-President Bacharuddin Jusuf Habibie, recommitted the country to the IMF package.

The Indonesian, Malaysian, Thai and Philippine economies contracted by 13.7%, 6.8%, 8% and 0.5% respectively in 1998. Growth in Singapore was just 1.5%. By late 1998, the daily volatility of crisis had given way to a second challenge, as it became clearer that Southeast Asia's economies would only recover slowly. The Indonesian economy faces further contraction in 1999, while the Philippines, Malaysia, Singapore and Thailand may stagnate, or grow slightly.

Although ASEAN made little direct contribution to the economic success of its members, it has been deeply affected by the region's economic problems. Expectations were high, both inside and outside the Association, that it would respond effectively to the crisis. Its failure to do so revealed that ASEAN's reputation rested, at least partly, on the economic success of its members. This had been based on commonality, rather than cooperation. Given the primacy of national sovereignty in ASEAN, discussion, let alone co-ordination, of economic policy had

ASEAN had no effective response to the economic crisis

been negligible. As the Association's Secretary-General, Rodolfo Severino, acknowledged in 1998, the crisis had affected both ASEAN's international reputation and its self-image.[12] Economic adversity has also complicated ASEAN's rules-based programme of economic integration, as new members waver over their commitments to reform, and has greatly reduced trade and investment flows between old members and new. This economic contact was expected to build political cohesion within an enlarged ASEAN.

It took ASEAN five months to reach its first coordinated position on the crisis. In that time, Thailand acknowledged the need for domestic reform, while in Malaysia, Mahathir argued that the crisis was the result of a Western conspiracy designed to reverse South-east Asia's progress.[13] ASEAN's first concrete response was to convene a meeting of its deputy finance ministers and their counterparts from the US, Japan, China, Hong Kong, South Korea and Australia, in Manila on 14 November 1997. The resulting Manila Framework, endorsed by ASEAN's heads of government at the APEC and ASEAN summits in November and December 1997, affirmed that individual countries bore primary responsibility for tackling the crisis through domestic reform, and that the IMF was the competent international body to assist where necessary. The Framework's most significant element was an agreement to create a surveillance mechanism within the Asian Development Bank (ADB), thereby helping ASEAN countries to exert 'peer pressure' on each other over macroeconomic and monetary policy. However, 18 months after the commitment was made, the machinery of this mechanism remained under discussion, reflecting differences within ASEAN over the benefits of this approach.

South-east Asia's economic crisis focused international attention on ASEAN's goal of a free-trade area. In December 1997, the Association's leaders reaffirmed the deadline of 2003 for tariff liberalisation among original members, 2006 for Vietnam and 2008 for Laos and Myanmar. In October 1998, Severino announced that 83% of tariff lines used in ASEAN countries were covered by AFTA, and that average tariff rates were down to 5.37%.[14] At the 1998 Hanoi summit, ASEAN belatedly announced so-called 'bold measures' on trade liberalisation, and changes to the investment regime for ASEAN and non-ASEAN investors. The AFTA deadline was brought forward to 2002. However, ASEAN lessened the impact of investment liberalisation by qualifying it as a short-term measure to be unevenly applied.

By April 1999, no ASEAN member had failed in its commitments to the AFTA schedule. The IMF packages for Thailand and Indonesia – the two most protected economies among original

ASEAN members – contain liberalisation demands that reinforce, or go substantially beyond, those in the AFTA schedule. Although liberalisation under these packages will take place on a Most Favoured Nation (MFN) basis, with new tariffs applying to all WTO members, rather than on a preferential, ASEAN-only basis, it will help to sustain momentum in AFTA.

Despite its increased political sensitivity, tariff liberalisation for ASEAN's original membership will probably remain on track. The economic crisis may, however, damage the liberalisation programmes of new members, which had reservations about them even before the downturn. Growth rates in Vietnam, Myanmar and Laos declined sharply in 1998, even though the non-convertibility of their currencies and restricted capital movement cushioned the impact of the crisis. New members were expected to continue moving towards greater economic openness, a process encouraged by trade liberalisation through AFTA. For Vietnam, Myanmar and Laos, however, their neighbours' experience has raised fears about the possible consequences of continued economic opening. In part because of the impact of the crisis, the transitional economies are thinking again about freer trade and investment regimes, and about deregulating domestic economic activity. The signals they have received from original members are mixed. On 1 September 1998, Malaysia imposed capital and currency controls, for example. Just as ASEAN was unable to impose discipline on its original membership in the first months of the crisis, so its rules-based programme of economic integration may not be enough to prevent new members from straying from the reform path.

The crisis has also damaged trade and investment flows between original and new ASEAN members, potentially affecting the Association's cohesion. Vietnam's exports to other ASEAN states fell by 31% in the first half of 1998, and, in the first nine months of 1998, its foreign-investment approvals (both ASEAN and non-ASEAN) declined by 58% over the same period in 1997.[15] Myanmar's approvals for the 1997–98 financial year were down by 53.6%.[16]

Indonesia's Transition

Indonesia's transition has region-wide ramifications that set it apart from the political impact of the economic crisis in other ASEAN countries. Indonesia is the region's largest state, with a geographic reach right across the southern flank of South-east Asia. Its population of over 200 million is more than twice that of ASEAN's next most populous country, Vietnam, and, until the economic crisis, it was the Association's largest economy. As ASEAN's *de facto* leader, Jakarta had contributed to the formation and implementation of the Association's guiding principles, and had played a major role in the Cambodian peace process, in South China Sea policy and in the enlargement agenda.

The reactions of its fellow ASEAN members to Indonesia's worsening economic and political situation in late 1997 demonstrated that they saw its future and that of the region as a whole as linked. No other South-east Asian state is regarded in this way. Chuan Leekpai's new government in Thailand used its good standing in Washington to urge flexibility in dealing with Indonesia, while accepting the strict conditions attached to its own financial-assistance package.[17] Singapore pledged $5bn to Jakarta's IMF package, and used its diplomatic capital in the West to urge governments there to pay greater attention to the country's problems. Even Brunei, with its low diplomatic profile, contributed to Indonesia's IMF package, and intervened to support the rupiah. Despite these efforts, the 'ASEAN way' limited what Indonesia's neighbours could do, contributing to the debate on 'non-interference' which took place following Suharto's resignation in May 1998.

Two specific problems emerged during the final months of Suharto's New Order: the toxic smog that engulfed Singapore, Malaysia, Brunei and southern Thailand in September 1997; and the breakdown in relations between Jakarta and the IMF in early 1998. At its worst, the smog, the result of land-clearance and climatic conditions caused by the *El Niño* weather system, reduced visibility to five metres. It paralysed economic activity, damaged tourism, led to massive health problems and made air travel dangerous. The Singapore-based Economy and Environment Program for Southeast Asia has estimated that it cost Malaysia $310m, and Singapore $74m.[18]

The 1997 episode was only the worst instance of a recurring problem. In 1994 and 1995, ASEAN environment ministers agreed that the region should be regarded as 'one eco-system', and that its members should cooperate in tackling cross-border pollution.[19] The plan left decisions about preventive action to national governments, and was severely compromised by the lack of monitoring of states' compliance. The 1997 pollution revealed the ineffectiveness of this approach. Affected countries nonetheless endured the disaster with little comment, silenced by Indonesia's regional weight and by the ASEAN principle of non-interference. In the wake of the 1997 smog, Association ministers and officials met with increasing frequency, and adopted a Regional Haze Action Plan. However, the plan focused on monitoring fires and pollution, and on fire-fighting; decisions on preventive steps were left to individual governments.

Similar limitations on ASEAN's ability to discuss issues of common concern were evident when the breakdown in Indonesia's relations with the IMF threatened a new wave of economic 'contagion'. Between October 1997 and February 1998, Singaporean Prime Minister Goh visited Indonesia three times to encourage Jakarta to keep to its IMF programme; Mahathir delivered the same message during his trip to the country in January 1998. Although these representations were made possible by links established through ASEAN, and paralleled the work of other world leaders, ASEAN heads nonetheless publicly denied that their attempts to discuss Indonesia's economic choices breached the non-interference principle. Below leadership level, and in ASEAN's myriad formal meetings, the subject of Indonesia's upheaval was strictly taboo.

The end of the Suharto era heralded a significant opening of Indonesian society, with the formation of new political parties, increased media freedom, the organisation of labour, the release of political prisoners, investigation of alleged abuses by the army and police, and the decision to allow East Timor to determine demo-cratically whether it would remain part of Indonesia. The elections on 7 June 1999 were to be the first in 40 years in which the outcome was not known in advance. Although Indonesia has retained a strong presidential system following Suharto's fall, the resulting government may be unstable. Indonesia has made remarkable progress in political and economic reform since May 1998, but the process remains difficult. The combination of economic crisis and loosened social controls has led to an upsurge in social, religious and ethnic tensions. Secessionist tendencies have emerged in a number of provinces.

Indonesia's size and strategic position justify a high level of international effort to assist its political regeneration and economic recovery. International financial institutions and key bilateral donors have played a prominent role in stabilising the country's economy. Western donors have backed the democratic-reform process by providing election funding and technical assistance, and by publicly encouraging change. A high degree of international involvement has also benefited progress towards resolving East Timor's status. Australia's call in December 1998 for East Timorese self-determination after a period of autonomy, for example, helped to move the Habibie government towards the decision to give East Timor a choice on its status; in April 1999, a vote on autonomy was set for 8 August.[20] Both the UN and Portugal, East Timor's former

Indonesia is set to remain vital but unstable

colonial ruler, are closely involved in consulting with Indonesia over this process. By contrast, ASEAN has avoided commenting on East Timor since its incorporation into Indonesia in 1976, and has not sought a role in discussions over the territory since January 1999. Individual ASEAN members may become involved in international efforts, but the non-interference principle and the political sensitivity of the issue will continue to limit the Association's participation as an institution.

Indonesia's decision to allow East Timor to determine its status by popular consultation may ultimately lead to the formation of a new independent nation in South-east Asia. If East Timor does become independent, it may be a candidate for ASEAN membership. Xanana Gusmão, the leader of East Timor's independence movement, the *Frente Revolucionario Timorense de Libertação e Independência* (FRETILIN), has stated that the territory should join the Association, as well as the 16-member South Pacific Forum.[21] Sections of élite opinion in Jakarta believe that, if the territory chooses independence, Indonesia should promote its ASEAN membership in order to ease its absorption into the region.[22]

Transitional Indonesia could pose a range of problems for its neighbours. These include a return of the smog; illegal population flows; violence against ethnic-Chinese Indonesians; and renewed destabilisation of the rupiah. The capacity of the post-election government to avert a recurrence of the smog may be limited and, given the economic crisis, failure would be even more costly to both Malaysia and Singapore than it was in 1997. The treatment of Indonesia's ethnic-Chinese minority could strain relations between ASEAN members. Much of the violence and looting that preceded Suharto's resignation was directed against ethnic Chinese. ASEAN's original members have ethnic-Chinese populations of their own, and could find themselves under pressure to confront Jakarta should violence recur. Finally, worsening economic conditions or communal tensions could prompt an outflow of illegal immigrants to Malaysia, Singapore or other ASEAN states. As illegal immigration rose with the onset of Indonesia's economic crisis, Kuala Lumpur imposed an abrupt repatriation programme, albeit with an understanding from Indonesia that the move would not be interpreted as antagonistic. According to traditional practice, ASEAN countries would respond to such developments bilaterally. However, mass movements of foreign populations simultaneously affecting a number of ASEAN members would suggest a regional-management role for the Association.

Debating Non-Interference

From 1997, the challenges posed by enlargement, economic crisis and upheavals in Indonesia prompted both outside commentators and ASEAN's original members to question whether the Association had the right tools to be a regional manager. Many external commentators concluded that the 'ASEAN way' had failed; some ASEAN members became increasingly disillusioned with the Association's role, and concerned that it was unprepared for the region's looming challenges.[23] Debate focused on ASEAN's principle of non-interference, and the related issues of its weak institutionalisation and reliance on consensus decision-making. Enlargement had led to some changes in the consensus approach before July 1997. In 1995, for example, ASEAN members agreed that a 'consensus minus' principle could apply to economic decision-making, whereby the Association could take positions on issues without a consensus provided that the interests of hesitant countries were not affected. This debate was, however, conducted without urgency, and with a reluctance to question the key tenets of the 'ASEAN way'.

ASEAN's apparent helplessness in the face of Cambodia's deteriorating political situation in early 1997 opened the debate on non-interference. Two weeks after Hun Sen's coup, Malaysia's then Acting Prime Minister, Anwar Ibrahim, published an article contending that ASEAN's 'non-involvement in the reconstruction of Cambodia actually contributed to the deterioration and final collapse of national reconciliation'.[24] Anwar argued that South-east Asian interdependence meant that 'the threat of spillovers of domestic, economic, social and political upheavals can seriously undermine the stability of the entire region', necessitating what he called 'constructive intervention'. This could involve assistance in electoral processes, a commitment to legal and administrative reforms, and the strengthening of civil society and the rule of law.

the failure to agree on 'constructive intervention'

Anwar's model of constructive intervention drew on post-Cold War developments in thinking about sovereignty and non-intervention, including the international response to the proliferation of 'failed states' and the increased foreign-policy salience of human rights and democracy.[25] But his proposal was also qualified in two important ways: the affected state would need to invite ASEAN's involvement, and the intervention would be political and economic, rather than military.[26] The first caveat provided some support for the assertion that constructive intervention would be consistent with the principle of non-interference.

Anwar's proposal elicited no response from ASEAN governments until June 1998, when Thai Foreign Minister Surin Pitsuwan called for a reassessment of the non-interference principle. By this time, the causes for concern with ASEAN's performance had multiplied with the spreading Indonesian smog and the deepening economic crisis. Under the Thai proposal, dubbed 'flexible engagement', ASEAN countries would be able to offer constructive criticism and advice to another member, if that state's actions affected another country or offended its principles.[27] This implied a definition of intervention that encompassed human rights. Anwar had earlier indicated that human-rights issues or a regime's political ideology were not excluded from his concept of constructive intervention: 'each country must find its own path to civil society. Yet, there are core humanitarian values we are bound by. In this sense, all of us in the region are our brother's keepers'.[28]

Surin's proposal marked a fundamental move away from non-interference as it had been practised in ASEAN. It therefore went beyond the kind of *ad hoc* initiatives with which the Association had responded to the Cambodian coup and the economic downturn. Flexible engagement set out a broad set of circumstances – beyond those outlined by Anwar – under which digression from the principle of non-interference could, according to the proposal, be justified. The 'dividing line between domestic affairs on the one hand and external or transnational issues on the other' was 'becoming blurred':

> *Many 'domestic' affairs have obvious external or transnational dimensions, adversely affecting neighbours, the region and the region's relations with others. In such cases, the affected countries should be able to express their opinions and concerns in an open, frank and constructive manner, which is not, and should not be, considered 'interference' in fellow-members' domestic affairs.*[29]

At its core, flexible engagement appeared to imply that ASEAN would act as a forum for members to comment on the behaviour of their neighbours, where this behaviour had a cross-border impact, or where it affected ASEAN's diplomatic credibility. Criticism would aim to pressure the state concerned into changing its policy, and would also allow countries to suggest solutions to problems. The proposal did not indicate that ASEAN should commit itself to EU-style integration under a supranational body. Nonetheless, given the broad range of policy areas covered by ASEAN, changing its operating principles would have transformed South-east Asian regionalism. According to the proposal:

> *ASEAN countries should have sufficient self-confidence in one another, both to discuss all issues once considered 'taboos' with one another with candour and sincerity, and to speak out on such issues in good faith when necessary and appropriate.*

Surin did not try to define the boundary between domestic affairs and issues that justified discussion by neighbours. ASEAN's recent experience suggested that this could be controversial. Economic contagion implied that the macroeconomic policies of one member could impinge on another. Political actions in Myanmar had caused the EU to cancel meetings, arguably to the detriment of other ASEAN countries, thereby apparently justifying others to pass comment on Myanmar's political situation.

Thailand's proposal won the backing of ASEAN Secretary-General Severino.[30] The Philippines, like Thailand one of the region's more liberal democracies, also supported it. Philippine Foreign Minister Siazon argued in July 1998 that 'any political upheaval in an ASEAN member country will have security, political and economic impacts on neighbouring countries'.[31] Manila is subject to domestic pressure to address human-rights issues in other ASEAN states and, having accepted Indonesian help to address problems in its Muslim-separatist south, has fewer qualms about criticism or intervention by its ASEAN peers.

Flexible engagement was debated and essentially rejected at ASEAN's Ministerial Meeting on 24–25 July 1998. Several factors determined this outcome. The first was Indonesia's conservative approach. Change was inconceivable while Suharto, ASEAN's elder statesman, held power. Proponents of flexible engagement may have expected the reformist government of his successor, Habibie, to take a different view, but Foreign Minister and ASEAN veteran Ali Alatas robustly defended the non-interference principle at the July meeting. In Malaysia, calls for ASEAN reform, which originated from Anwar, had no support from Mahathir. While in Singapore influential voices were arguing for ASEAN's greater insti-

the restricted debate on 'flexible engagement'

tutionalisation and a faster decision-making process, there was no wish to alienate Jakarta during its uncertain transition.[32] Opponents of flexible engagement argued that the non-interference principle was enshrined in the UN Charter, and hence governed all inter-state relations. However, this position ignored the particular interpretation of non-interference developed within ASEAN, which proscribed certain forms of problem-solving and communication between states in the pursuit of qualitatively deeper integration.

ASEAN's enlargement was the second factor working against change. Altering the non-interference principle would have amounted to changing the rules of the club after admitting new members who had joined precisely because they accepted the old ones. ASEAN's new membership has strongly objected to any change. Vietnam has supported a *stricter* application of non-interference than ASEAN has hitherto practised, avoiding even private pressure on Myanmar. Myanmar's tolerance of bilateral pressure does not suggest that it would accept a revision of the principle of non-interference. The nature of the regime means that it would be an early target of a more interventionist ASEAN approach. Further justification would be given by the spillover of its civil war into Thailand, by the regime's treatment of ethnic and religious minorities, and by the country's drug production. Both Myanmar and Laos reacted to Thailand's flexible-engagement proposal by calling in the Thai ambassadors in their respective capitals. Although outside ASEAN at the time of the debate, Hun Sen declared that the non-interference principle was key to Cambodia's participation in ASEAN, and that 'any attempts to revise this principle will pose a threat to the strength and confidence in this regional association'.[33]

The formal debate on flexible engagement at the July 1998 meeting concluded with an announcement that the Association would henceforth practice 'enhanced interaction'. This was a new term apparently meaning that ASEAN could have more open exchanges on issues with clearly defined cross-border effects – such as piracy or the smog – while respecting the principle of non-interference. This is effectively an uneasy truce between the Association's conservatives and its, albeit tentative, forces for change. According to Severino, 'enhanced interaction' is an expression of the incremental change taking place in the way ASEAN operates: 'one can expect interactions within ASEAN to be more intensive and more free'.[34] Severino has also suggested that:

> ASEAN may have to move toward the greater use of more
> formal instruments and binding commitments in the future,
> as developments like the financial and economic crisis and the
> rise of such transboundary problems as the pollution of the

sea and air press ASEAN's members to ever closer co-
ordination, cooperation and integration.[35]

It is far from clear that incremental change is a workable solution to an issue of such fundamental importance. Several ASEAN members are deeply opposed to such change, and have a vested interest in resisting it. Some new members have already baulked at the transparency measures required as part of ASEAN's economic-surveillance mechanism. It is questionable how effective enhanced interaction will be in exerting pressure on governments, while ASEAN's organisational culture is ingrained and unlikely to change without a clear signal from the group's leadership.

The enhanced-interaction compromise has not laid the intervention issue to rest. Immediately after its announcement, Siazon suggested that the people of Myanmar should stage a bloodless revolution, to which the government-controlled media responded with accusations that Manila was a 'lackey of the West'.[36] Surin claimed that, since his position on non-intervention was well known, ASEAN states would understand if he criticised them.[37] Thailand and the Philippines have been involved in a 'contact group' of nations, including the US, Japan, the UK and Australia, exploring ways to use aid as a leverage for political reform in Myanmar.

The challenges to non-interference have not come exclusively from those countries arguing for change in July 1998. Following Anwar's dismissal by Mahathir and his arrest in late 1998, both Indonesia and the Philippines breached the principle. Both heads of state discussed Anwar during a bilateral meeting on 13 October 1998 and, moreover, publicised the fact that they had done so. Both publicly expressed concern over his treatment, and it was strongly suggested that Habibie cancelled a visit to Malaysia over the issue. Alatas took care to explain that Jakarta's response did not constitute a break with ASEAN's principles, but this did not stop Kuala Lumpur from issuing a diplomatic protest.[38] In February 1999, in another significant departure from past practice, Goh called on Jakarta to hold elections that would be accepted as fair and legitimate by the Indonesian people.[39]

The debate over non-interference has revealed how far the expectations of ASEAN have changed since 1967. At its formation, the Association's purpose was exclusively political and security-related. All of its cooperation was a means to these political and security ends. Thirty years on, ASEAN had embarked on a process of economic integration, which was expected to produce economic outcomes – albeit not ones that would redefine the South-east Asian economy. ASEAN had become the world's most institutionalised regional association apart from the EU, cooperating in every field of public policy and requiring a massive investment of national resources by its membership. Cooperation on issues such as cross-border pollution raised expectations that ASEAN could have a problem-solving role.

Outside South-east Asia, ASEAN has tried to speak with one voice in diplomatic discussions. Following the end of the Cold War, these discussions have increasingly included political conditions within states, human rights and economic choices. The Association, through its 'Vision 2020' statement delivered at the 1997 summit, espoused a view of 'one Southeast Asia', a 'community of caring societies … bound by a common regional identity'. Yet ASEAN has refused to impose political or economic conditions on membership, and cannot guarantee that all of its members are moving towards economic openness and 'government with the consent and greater participation of the people'.[40] The debate on non-interference highlights the tension between those states wishing to preserve ASEAN's self-imposed limitations, and the more expansive claims which the Association has made for itself.

ASEAN's ambitious enlargement began at a time when its members were enjoying political and economic stability, and relatively good relations with each other. It was nonetheless expected to test the Association's cohesion. That strain is now much more pronounced given the upheaval in core ASEAN countries. Members have little energy to devote to the integration of Vietnam, Myanmar, Laos and Cambodia. Indonesia's domestic preoccupations mean that it is distracted from ASEAN issues, making consensus-building more difficult. The non-interference debate, occurring in the midst of the enlargement process, has made new members suspicious. It has underlined ASEAN's political diversity and the wide variety of expectations among its members. Never before has political orientation been so directly reflected in approaches to the Association. While the debate led to a 'consensus', a number of ASEAN's original members find this arrangement difficult to accept and are testing its limits. The Association is hamstrung in conducting its affairs in a more integrationist way when this approach does not have the full support of the membership.

chapter 3

ASEAN and the Asia-Pacific

In the early post-Cold War period, ASEAN pursued an active diplomatic agenda. It supported the concept of an Asia-Pacific community premised on US strategic, political and economic engagement, and on recognition of China as a major power, with attendant rights and responsibilities. It played a leading procedural role in the ARF, endorsed APEC and initiated ASEM. It also explored, albeit inconclusively, the possibility of opening a pan-Asian dialogue. The enlargement process was intended to maintain ASEAN's diplomatic centrality by allowing it to speak for 'one South-east Asia' and its 500m people. However, the strains on ASEAN exerted by enlargement, the economic crisis and Indonesia's difficulties mean that its role in the Asia-Pacific, and its relations with major regional powers, need to be reassessed.

China

Beijing welcomed the prospect of ASEAN-10, stating that it would, as then Foreign Minister Qian put it, be 'more closely connected to China'.[1] China's claims in the South China Sea made it the only major power to pose a direct challenge to the territorial interests of South-east Asian countries, and ASEAN expected to emerge from enlargement better able to command the attention and respect of its massive neighbour. However, while enlargement increased ASEAN's weight in terms of population, as well as economically, this would not automatically gain Beijing's respect. Expansion, together with economic crisis and upheaval in Indonesia, make it more difficult for ASEAN to present itself as a cohesive force, and complicate its efforts to forge a common approach to China.

ASEAN's most important challenge in its relations with Beijing is to achieve a coherent position over the territorial claims in the South China Sea. Despite differences in its members' perceptions of the potential threat posed by China, there was sufficient common ground for the Association to censure Beijing in 1995 over its occupation of Mischief Reef, and to call for restraint based on the 1992 Manila Declaration.[2] ASEAN's consensus made it possible for the ARF, augmented by Washington, to call for the peaceful settlement of claims in the South China Sea. Had ASEAN not protested, Washington would have been constrained in its response given its 'neutral' position that the South China Sea is a disputed territory.

ASEAN's admission of Vietnam made it easier for the Association to take a firm stand over the South China Sea – indeed, members were concerned that Vietnam's often poor relations with China could hamper efforts to engage Beijing, and could lead to entanglement in bilateral disputes. Vietnam has handled these concerns with some dexterity, and has improved its relations with China. While it continues to do so, Hanoi will be unwilling to disrupt the relationship between ASEAN and Beijing, although it is testing the limits of the Association's support for its claims to the Paracel Islands, which were seized by China from disintegrating South Vietnamese control in 1974, and to the Gulf of Tonkin.[3] It has suited Vietnam to regard the Manila Declaration as applicable to these issues, whereas other ASEAN countries see grounds for differentiating between the dispute over the Spratly Islands, which involves multiple claims, and those over the Gulf of Tonkin and the Paracels, which are purely bilateral. Indonesia, the Philippines and Vietnam protested when Beijing, on ratifying the UN Convention on the Law of the Sea (UNCLOS), defined controversial baselines for the Paracels in May 1996.[4] ASEAN itself belatedly asked only for an explanation of the process by which China had arrived at these baselines.

In admitting Myanmar without a guaranteed way of weakening its reliance on Beijing, ASEAN gambled with the organisation's capacity to reach consensus on responses to Chinese

Map 2 *Maritime Claims in the South China Sea*

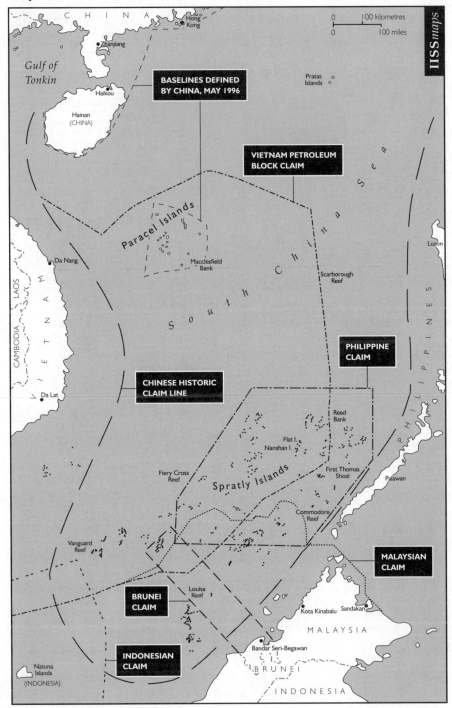

Map 3 *The Spratly and Paracel Islands*

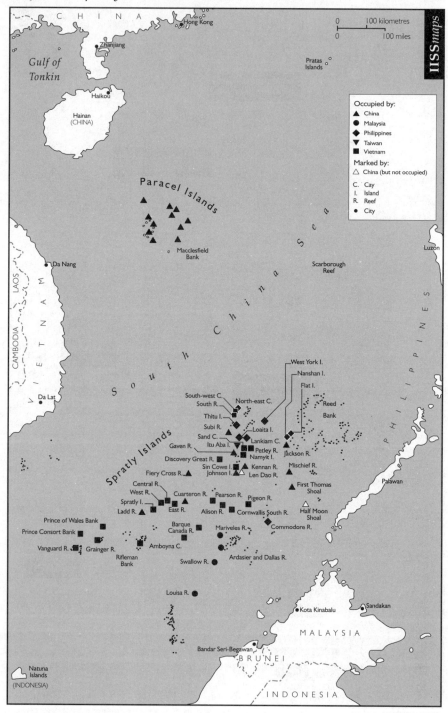

IISSmaps

Occupied by:
▲ China
● Malaysia
◆ Philippines
▼ Taiwan
■ Vietnam

Marked by:
△ China (but not occupied)

C. Cay
I. Island
R. Reef
● City

assertiveness in the South China Sea. Myanmar does not have claims there, diminishing its right to speak on the issue. Given Beijing's support for the Yangon regime, Myanmar could be reluctant to join any ASEAN consensus to censure China, or could be pressured by Beijing into not doing so. Laos and Cambodia, as non-claimants with positive but less dependent relationships with Beijing, would be unlikely to challenge the positions of claimant states.

Between 1995 and late 1998, China exercised restraint over the Spratly Islands, while continuing to test its claims to the Gulf of Tonkin. Beijing did not define baselines for the Spratlys when it ratified UNCLOS, for example. China gradually accepted that the South China Sea would have a place in its dialogue with ASEAN, marking a shift away from the strict bilateralism that it had pursued before 1995. At the 1997 ASEAN–China summit, President Jiang Zemin agreed that all parties 'should explore ways for cooperation in the areas concerned'.[5] In October 1998, however, Beijing reinforced the structures that it had built on Mischief Reef in 1995. Although less provocative than seizing territory, the timing of the move appeared calculated to capitalise on ASEAN's difficulties; as Severino put it, the Association had 'bigger problems to deal with, particularly the economy'.[6] ASEAN's response at its summit with China in December 1998 was muted, although some countries did raise the matter bilaterally.

In terms of the other two challenges facing ASEAN – economic crisis and Indonesia's transition – China's conduct has sent generally positive signals. By the end of 1998, South-east Asia had suffered substantially more than China from the region's economic crisis. ASEAN's fears that Beijing would devalue the yuan, thereby deepening the malaise, have not been realised. Although the issue was high on the agenda in discussions with China in 1997 and 1998, Beijing's decision not to devalue has been based more on calculations about the state of the Chinese economy, than on concern not to destabilise South-east Asia. Nonetheless, its first-ever contribution to an IMF package demonstrated both that Beijing saw benefits in its neighbours' stability, and that it accepted the Fund's authority. Similarly, China has been sensitive to South-east Asian concerns in its response to Indonesia's upheaval. Its restraint following anti-Chinese rioting, for example, was a far cry from the interventionist role it played in the 1960s. When ethnic Chinese were targeted in unrest in 1965–66, Beijing dispatched ships to evacuate refugees. In May 1998, the government stated that issues relating to ethnic Chinese in Indonesia were Jakarta's affair, and called on it to protect 'Chinese and other ethnic groups'.[7]

Overall, China's actions since July 1997 indicate that it sees little benefit in a destabilised South-east Asia, and is prepared to take steps, albeit modest ones, to help the region economically. This does not mean that an enlarged ASEAN has strengthened its claim to Beijing's respect. On the contrary: China sees the Association, beset with economic troubles and deprived of Indonesia's leadership, as *less* strategically coherent and purposeful. Beijing's reinforcement of Mischief Reef in October 1998 was an opportunistic action, suggesting a change in the constraints Beijing feels in pursuit of its long-held goals in the South China Sea.

Japan

While supporting US strategic, political and economic engagement in Asia, ASEAN has seen itself as a potential kingmaker, prodding Japan towards political and economic leadership. Tokyo's readiness to assume such a role is a precondition for any pan-Asian grouping. Japan has, however, recognised the potential conflict between Asian leadership and its support for the US in Asia, complicating efforts to respond to ASEAN's overtures.

ASEAN's enlargement laid the basis for closer relations, given Tokyo's explicit and, among the Association's Western partners, unique, encouragement of ASEAN-10. Japan did not ask the Association to exclude Myanmar, and its bilateral approach to the Yangon regime is less punitive than that of other Western powers. For

Japan, not ASEAN, led on Cambodia

example, it provides aid on the basis of case-by-case approval. Myanmar's admission into ASEAN has not disrupted Tokyo's dialogue partnership with the Association in any respect. While Tokyo has asked ASEAN countries individually to press Myanmar to reform, it has not used Japan–ASEAN fora to do so. Tokyo's efforts to normalise Cambodia's international status also were consistent with its encouragement of ASEAN-10. Ironically, Japan's Four Pillars proposal, which paved the way for elections in

Cambodia, was an example of Japanese leadership in Asia – but on a matter which it was ASEAN's responsibility to manage. As a result, Tokyo did not receive widespread recognition for its initiative, either from within South-east Asia, or from outside it. Japan encouraged ASEAN to admit Cambodia at the summit in December 1998, before all ASEAN members had agreed on the timing.

While ASEAN's enlargement laid the basis for closer cooperation, the economic crisis has strained the relationship. Japan, like other Western powers, has lowered its opinion of ASEAN's economic competence, while the Association itself has been disappointed by Japan's response to the crisis, which was widely seen as a leadership opportunity. Japan's attempt in October 1997 to create an Asian Monetary Fund – which would have supplanted the IMF in providing funds to ailing economies – won the backing of some ASEAN countries, but not of the US and key European states, which saw it as undercutting the IMF and removing the Fund's strict conditionality. Tokyo swiftly agreed, and channelled its financial support for the region's ailing economies through existing international institutions. The episode served as a reminder of the difficulties Japan, a major US ally, faced in trying to pursue a leadership role in Asia.

In terms of its financial contributions at least, Japan appears to have met ASEAN's demands to demonstrate its commitment to South-east Asia. Tokyo pledged $9bn to the IMF packages for Indonesia and Thailand, and committed $30bn to ailing Asian economies including South Korea in October 1998. Smaller sums were committed at the 1998 APEC and ASEAN summits. But ASEAN also pressed Tokyo, the region's largest investor and a major trading partner, to introduce domestic economic reform to reinvigorate Japan's economy, and to strengthen its financial sector. The Association made an unusually direct request for action at the Post-Ministerial Conference in July 1998. This followed coordinated pressure on Tokyo by the US, and by China, which argued that it would be unable to resist devaluing the yuan unless Japan defended the yen. Tokyo's response to the economic crisis was criticised within ASEAN as tardy, and its readiness to provide funding contrasted with its reluctance to undertake reforms at home, or to push ahead with Asia-Pacific trade liberalisation.[8]

Japan's defensiveness over its economic performance limited its manoeuvrability in responding to ASEAN's request for a meeting of all Association and North Asian leaders at the 1998 ASEAN summit.[9] The request was a reinterpretation of then Prime Minister Ryutaro Hashimoto's attempt in January 1997 to create a broader agenda with ASEAN by extending Tokyo's relationship beyond its economic base. The Association accepted Hashimoto's proposal for regular summits, and then offered similar summits to China and South Korea. To coincide with the first of these meetings in December 1997, Mahathir hosted a celebratory gathering of all ASEAN and North Asian leaders. Hanoi repeated the 'pan-Asian formula' at the 1998 ASEAN summit. In July 1997, Beijing had praised the Association for proposing the summit with China, Japan and South Korea, describing it as 'a new channel for building up confidence and enhancing cooperation among East Asian nations'.[10] China's support for 'ASEAN plus three' meetings means that there is pressure on Japan to accept future invitations to attend meetings of this kind.

The United States

Despite Washington's campaign to discourage ASEAN from admitting Myanmar – Secretary of State Madeleine Albright once referred to SLORC as 'an ugly acronym for an ugly government' – Yangon's inclusion has not significantly altered the US–ASEAN relationship. Although there was some understanding in Washington of ASEAN's interest in reducing China's influence in Myanmar, US policy was primarily determined by human-rights concerns. Albright wrote to all of her South-east Asian counterparts over the issue of Yangon's inclusion, and, once it had taken place, stated that 'Burma's problems now become ASEAN's problems'.[11] However, given the region's political and economic upheaval, broader issues of stability have weighed more heavily with Washington than has dismay at Myanmar's new status.[12] The US adopted a flexible approach to its meeting with ASEAN on 23–24 May 1998. The gathering involved senior officials from Myanmar and, although hosted by the US, was held in the Philippines to avoid visa problems.

Nonetheless, Washington's desire that critical issues of stability should not be hostage to its concerns about Myanmar does not mean that nothing has changed in its relations with ASEAN. A sticking-point will be Washington's refusal to allow officials from Myanmar to attend meetings in the US. Washington is likely to use the full range of ASEAN fora to raise its human-rights concerns in Myanmar, as well as in Cambodia. This is largely a post-Cold War development: human-rights concerns had hitherto been kept separate from the ASEAN agenda.

ASEAN's enlargement has broadened the range of strategic outlooks among its members, and could weaken the consensus on the benefits of US strategic engagement in Asia. ASEAN's approach to the US presence is still based on the legacy of cooperation during the Cold War. As the Association put it in May 1993, when the ARF was formed: 'The continuing presence of the United States ... would contribute to regional stability'.[13] In 1998, Indonesian Foreign Minister Alatas marked two decades of the dialogue partnership between ASEAN and the US thus: 'the United States has also played a leading role [in the Asia-Pacific] in continuing reiteration of its commitment to security'.[14]

ASEAN's position on US engagement is to an extent premised on its members' bilateral defence relationships with Washington. These include alliances with the Philippines and Thailand, and Singapore's provision of extensive defence access. In Indonesia's case, Jakarta's support for US strategic engagement in Asia remained steady under Suharto, despite frequent problems in the bilateral relationship, including over defence links. Enlargement has, however, brought into the Association countries lacking strong bilateral ties to *significant differences over the US role* underpin their strategic outlook. Washington has begun defence relations with Vietnam and Laos but these will, for historical reasons, develop slowly. Hanoi's fear of China's emergence as an unrivalled power in Asia gives Hanoi no interest in seeing a decline in US strategic engagement, although the ways in which it can give practical or rhetorical support to Washington's presence are limited. Myanmar's alignment with Beijing, and Washington's opposition to the SPDC regime, suggests that Yangon does not support the US presence. Myanmar could use ZOPFAN to oppose ASEAN statements backing Washington's security role in Asia, but, as a new member with limited credibility, it is unlikely to take this route unless serious divisions appeared among the original membership.

The region's economic crisis has reaffirmed Washington's economic and political role in Asia; the US has been described as the 'indispensable co-architect' of the IMF's programmes.[15] It contributed $8bn to the packages for Indonesia and South Korea, and senior administration officials such as Treasury Secretary Robert Rubin have been closely involved in the international response to the crisis. Washington hosted a visit by Thai Prime Minister Chuan Leekpai in March 1998 in a bid to boost his authority and make it easier for him to implement reforms. Clinton's preoccupation with the inquiry by Special Prosecutor Kenneth Starr notwithstanding, the US was generally regarded as having played a unique leadership role in the first year of the crisis. ASEAN's original membership either generally supported or sought to increase this involvement, suggesting that the crisis had reaffirmed the Association's support for US engagement. Bangkok, for example, 'regretted' the US decision not to contribute individually to Thailand's IMF package, and welcomed subsequent assurances that Washington remained engaged in the region. Singapore lobbied for US attention to Indonesia's problems and, in November 1998, announced that it would allow Washington to use its new naval base at Changi, as well as building a pier specifically for US warships.

Despite this general backing for the US role in tackling the economic crisis, there were also more negative undercurrents. Just as the 'East Asian miracle' gave rise in some quarters to pan-Asianist sentiment, and to calls for commensurate institutions, so shared resentment at the economic crisis and consequent IMF prescriptions could encourage a different kind of pan-Asianism. A year into the crisis, for example, Malaysia reiterated its call for an exclusively East Asian grouping.[16] Kuala Lumpur may have viewed the ASEAN summits of December 1997 and 1998, which were attended by North Asian leaders, as a basis for formalised 'ASEAN plus three' summitry. In promoting this idea, Mahathir accused the US of using APEC to 'expand its domination' of the Asia-Pacific.[17] Mahathir's comments reflected disapproval of US Vice-President Al Gore's speech at a gala business event during the Kuala Lumpur APEC meetings, in which Gore backed reform movements in various Asian countries, and implicitly criticised Anwar's imprisonment.[18] Gore's support for the 'brave people' calling for reform in Malaysia was widely criticised in the region as a bombastic display which distracted APEC from its crucial economic agenda. Mahathir also promoted the idea that 'the West' had engineered the economic crisis to punish Asia for its success. Referring to the nineteenth-century cooperation between the UK, France, the US, Russia and Japan which opened Chinese markets, Mahathir claimed that virtually the same countries were again working together to force open Asian markets:

> there will be no occupation of the territories but already we are seeing how the choice of leaders of these countries can be influenced by pressures on the currency. The effect is much the same. In fact it is really much cheaper and even profitable to use this financial pressure in order to achieve the effect of colonisation.[19]

Despite the anguish which the economic crisis has caused in South-east Asia, perceptions of what triggered it, and of the roles of the major players, vary. Most countries in the region recognise the importance of internal economic weaknesses, as well as external factors. Countries under IMF programmes are particularly aware of the importance of US support for the Fund, and of the significance of the American market to their prospects for recovery. Increased strategic uncertainty would generally lead Asia's capitals to regard the US commitment as more, rather than less, important.

Ultimately, Indonesia's assessment of the benefits of US engagement in Asia will determine whether ASEAN maintains its enthusiasm for the Asia-Pacific despite its new strategic diversity and the potential for a backlash against Washington or the IMF. Indonesian economist Mari Pangestu summed up the feeling in her country in June 1998, when she argued that suggestions that Washington and the IMF had precipitated Suharto's departure were an insult to the domestic reform movement.[20] Jakarta has been a key backer of US engagement, despite occasional bilateral turbulence. A sustained effort by the US to assist the Indonesian economy, while exercising restraint over political prescriptions during the country's transition, is the best basis for a strong bilateral relationship, and hence continuity in ASEAN's approach to the broader region.

ASEAN and Asia-Pacific Institutions

In the early post-Cold War period, ASEAN's appetite for Asia-Pacific issues derived from South-east Asia's relative stability. The Association instigated the ARF, and retains a leading procedural role within it. Despite its strong rhetorical support, ASEAN does not have a similarly prominent role in APEC. The strains on the Association will accordingly have a varied impact on its institutional commitments in the Asia-Pacific.

The ARF

The ARF has wide support among its original members, and continues to attract new expressions of interest; Mongolia became its twenty-second member in July 1998. It has nonetheless been unable to make its planned progression from confidence-building to preventive diplomacy. It is also navigating a difficult course between conventional security, and new foreign-policy issues encompassing political stability, human rights and 'comprehensive' security, including the impact of the economic crisis.

ASEAN acts as a caucus within the ARF, and so its ability to reach consensus on strategic issues is important to how they are treated within the Forum at large. ASEAN's expansion has political

Table 3 *ARF Membership*

(Date joined)		
Brunei (1994)	**Cambodia** (1995)	**Indonesia** (1994)
Laos (1994)	**Malaysia** (1994)	**Myanmar** (1996)
Philippines (1994)	**Singapore** (1994)	**Thailand** (1994)
Vietnam (1994)		
Australia (1994)	Canada (1994)	China (1994)
EU (1994)	India (1996)	Japan (1994)
South Korea (1994)	Mongolia (1998)	New Zealand (1994)
Papua New Guinea (1994)	Russia (1994)	US (1994)

and operational implications for the regional security dialogue because the Association's greater diversity of strategic outlook could make it more difficult to reach agreement on issues of substance. At an institutional level, ASEAN's enlargement has rekindled the issue of its capacity – and right – to chair the ARF. New members intend to take up their chairing responsibilities when alphabetical rotation begins in 2001, with Cambodia assuming the ASEAN chair in 2002, and hosting the ARF in 2003. While the admission of Myanmar, Cambodia and Laos into the ARF was accepted without reference to their domestic political situations, membership and chairing are not equivalent functions. The Association has admitted countries whose credentials for contributing to the development of a regional security dialogue are questionable. The limited organisational capacity of ASEAN's new members means that they may be unable to ensure that progress is made during their year as chair. The chair of the ARF's 1997 meeting, Malaysian Foreign Minister Badawi, was instrumental in obtaining agreement for the ARF to endorse ASEAN mediation in Cambodia. This raised expectations that a 'good-offices' role for the ARF chair could facilitate preventive diplomacy but, given the resource limitations and credibility questions concerning some of ASEAN's new members, this is unlikely to succeed. The region will need to confront the irony that, at least nominally, its weakest and least stable nations may assume responsibility for guiding the security dialogue, while its strongest and most stable ones cannot.

The ARF's approach to regional security was derived from ASEAN's security culture, although the terms assigned to it did not emerge from ASEAN's lexicon.[21] In 1995, the ARF approved three stages of development: confidence-building; preventive diplomacy; and the 'elaboration of approaches' to conflict. This was a modification of the term 'conflict-resolution mechanisms', which had appeared in the ASEAN Concept Paper provided to the ARF, but which was unacceptable to China. Reaching the third stage would see the Forum moving beyond ASEAN's approach to solving problems given that the Association's mechanism for resolving disputes under the TAC has never been invoked. Differences over how the ARF should develop reflect the desire of its Western participants for greater predictability in the ARF process, and a broader recognition that mechanisms appropriate for a small group of geographically proximate countries cannot be directly translated to the Asia-Pacific.

Despite the 1995 consensus on the road ahead, the important proviso that the dialogue would 'move at a pace comfortable to all participants' has given China a virtual right of veto over progress from stage to stage. The agreement that confidence-building measures and preventive diplomacy could proceed in tandem *'particularly* where the subject matter overlap [emphasis added]' has proved opaque, and has led only to an 'intention' to consider preventive diplomacy. China has resisted even this development, although Beijing is increasingly comfortable with confidence-building concepts, demonstrating its growing commitment to, and appreciation of, the multilateral security dialogue. Given the international praise that China has received for its responsible regional role during the economic crisis, it could be time to seek movement on preventive diplomacy. Issues relating

the perils of Chinese control of the 'comfort level'

to Taiwan are excluded from the ARF, and, because of North Korea's absence, the Forum is limited in its discussion of the Korean Peninsula. The Spratly Islands dispute would thus be a logical target of ARF preventive diplomacy. However, while prepared to tolerate expressions of concern and calls for restraint, China is wary of any aspirations the ARF may have to address this issue.

For a range of reasons, if ASEAN continues to chair the ARF, the dialogue could stagnate. The original ASEAN countries have less energy to devote to ARF issues, particularly those concerning North Asia. With the exception of Vietnam, the capacity of its new members to take forward a regional security dialogue is doubtful. Alternative chairing possibilities include rotating responsibility among all ARF members, with an ASEAN state taking every second turn, as is the case in APEC. This may introduce new problems because of the presence within the ARF of countries whose primary strategic focus is not the Asia-Pacific. Other options include co-chairing between an ASEAN and a non-ASEAN country, as in the ARF's intersessional meetings, or a rotating troika. These alternatives have little support in ASEAN governments, which argue that the Association is unique in its ability to engage both Washington and Beijing.

ASEAN's problems also have broader implications for the ARF. According to Jose Almonte, a national security adviser to former Philippine President Ramos:

> the 'ASEAN approach' that the ARF follows accentuates the positive — focusing not on controversy, but on areas of common interest from which multilateral cooperation can be developed and expanded. Divisive issues are simply passed over for later resolution — or until they have been made either irrelevant or innocuous by time and events.[22]

The perception of the Association's inadequacy in the face of challenges since July 1997, together with the debate over its operating methods, raise important questions for those who argue that the ARF should aim to prevent or solve security problems. Parallel issues include the diversity of the ARF's membership; the impact of its weak institutionalisation; its consensus decision-making (also known as 'the lowest-common-denominator' approach); and the way in which it defines 'political stability', 'human rights' and 'regional security'. As in ASEAN, the extent to which membership of the ARF modifies behaviour depends on the extent to which the country concerned subscribes to the Forum's aims, fears its criticism and is comfortable within it. The outcome is restraining, rather than problem-solving, suggesting that the ARF's progress towards preventive diplomacy or 'approaches to conflict' will be difficult. While it is useful for the ARF to test the limits of institution-building, the prospects that it will develop beyond dialogue to preventing or resolving conflict are clearly limited. Its most substantial contribution will be raising 'comfort levels' among an increasingly wide circle of players, and exerting some restraining influence in countries' approaches to issues of strategic concern.

APEC

Unlike the ARF, APEC does not rely on ASEAN as its 'driving force'. APEC is not chaired exclusively by ASEAN countries, nor does the ASEAN consensus necessarily determine the position which its

Table 4 *APEC Membership*

(Date joined)		
Brunei (1989)	**Indonesia** (1989)	**Malaysia** (1989)
Philippines (1989)	**Singapore** (1989)	**Thailand** (1989)
Vietnam (1998)		
Australia (1989)	Canada (1989)	China (1991)
Chile (1994)	Hong Kong SAR (1991)	Japan (1989)
South Korea (1989)	Mexico (1993)	New Zealand (1989)
Papua New Guinea (1993)	Peru (1998)	Russia (1998)
	Taiwan (1991)	US (1989)

Note   SAR = Special Administrative Region

members take in APEC. Strains within the Association are thus less likely to slow APEC's agenda. ASEAN's enlargement has under-scored the loose relationship between the Association and APEC since Cambodia, Laos and Myanmar will not be admitted before 2007 at the earliest. Its ASEAN colleagues strongly supported Vietnam's APEC membership, but the forum imposed a ten-year membership moratorium in December 1997 as a quid pro quo for admitting Vietnam, Peru and Russia. As a result of enlargement, ASEAN is divided in APEC, as it is in ASEM, between accepted countries – the original members, Brunei and Vietnam – and non-accepted ones.

While ASEAN's strains do not impinge on APEC *per se*, a halt to trade liberalisation in key ASEAN countries would clearly damage the forum, because liberalisation within ASEAN and within APEC is mutually reinforcing. AFTA's liberalisation target of 2003 for original members provides an interim goal for APEC's own deadline of 2020. As differing policy responses to the economic crisis develop, ASEAN's economic mainstream is under pressure. Although the Association's original members have reaffirmed their commitment to AFTA's liberalisation target, its success will be an indication of the region's ongoing commitment to liberalisation.

Table 5 *ASEM Participants*

Brunei	Indonesia	Malaysia
Philippines	Singapore	Thailand
Vietnam	China	EU
Japan	South Korea	

Beyond the Asia-Pacific

ASEAN's most significant relations outside the Asia-Pacific are with the EU. Europe's agreement to ASEM was indicative of the attention that ASEAN could command on the basis of its members' economic performance, its Cold War legacy of cooperation with the West and its role in establishing the ARF. However, bringing Myanmar into the grouping has seriously disrupted the Association's relationship with the EU. Far from guaranteeing ASEAN's diplomatic centrality, enlargement has substantially limited its diplomatic manoeuvrability in its dealings with Europe. For almost two years after the enlargement ceremony in Kuala Lumpur, which was boycotted by the UK, relations were badly disrupted. Given the problems in the relationship between ASEAN and the EU, greater emphasis has been placed on ASEM, which is not complicated by the issue of Myanmar since Yangon is not a participant. Ironically, however, Myanmar's absence, together with that of Laos and Cambodia, weakens ASEAN's identity in ASEM, as it does in APEC.

ASEAN's decision to admit Myanmar rested on a strategic calculation about Chinese influence, which it did not expect Washington or the EU to share. Nonetheless, ASEAN underestimated the strength of European reaction. Indonesian Foreign Minister Alatas indicated in September 1997 that, since Myanmar was a member of ASEAN, Yangon would automatically participate in all ASEAN–EU events. ASEAN was therefore unprepared for the EU's decision that Myanmar was not eligible to participate either in the official-level Joint Cooperation Committee meeting originally scheduled for

November 1997, or in the ASEAN–Europe Ministerial Meeting scheduled for March 1999, and due to be hosted by Europe.[23] Numerous attempts to reschedule the JCC have ended in disarray and, by April 1999, it still had not met. Although the officials' meeting was to be held in Thailand, removing any need for an EU country to issue visas to representatives from Myanmar, it falls under the auspices of a formal agreement to which Yangon is not a party, giving the EU technical grounds to refuse its participation. ASEAN in turn refused to attend in the country's absence. The Ministerial Meeting, which involved visa issues over which the EU would not make concessions, also did not go ahead as planned.

Problems over Myanmar are symptomatic of the way in which ASEAN's dialogue partnerships have changed with the end of the Cold War to take account of human-rights issues. There are, however, differences of approach between the EU and the US, which are largely attributable to Europe's limited strategic interests in South-east Asia. Washington's greater commitment led it to adopt a more flexible approach to ASEAN enlargement and the issue of Myanmar's membership. By the same token, ASEAN members have also not responded uniformly to the EU's position. Some have robustly defended Myanmar's prima-facie right, as an ASEAN member, to participate in all of the Association's meetings. However, in March 1999, the Philippines publicly called on Yangon to reform to facilitate its participation in the dialogue between ASEAN and the EU.

Far from underpinning its diplomatic centrality, enlargement has limited ASEAN's manoeuvrability in its relations with key Western partners, and diluted its identity in ASEM and APEC. At the same time, the credibility that ASEAN derived from the economic achievement of its members has dwindled. These developments do not mean that ASEAN will be sidelined in Western capitals. However, the emerging interest is merely in the role that ASEAN can play in confidence-building, minimising tensions at a time of great change in South-east Asia. This is far from the expectations of the early post-Cold War period.

ASEAN's historic enlargement to encompass the whole of Southeast Asia coincided with an unprecedented series of challenges. The decision to enlarge rapidly was taken when the original members were politically stable and enjoying strong economic growth, and when ASEAN's diplomatic standing was high. Just as enlargement was under way, the economic crisis broke, and Indonesia began its uncertain political transition. While it acknowledged that enlargement would slow its consensus decision-making, ASEAN did not have a way to reconcile its new breadth with its attempts to achieve a greater depth of integration. Nor did it adequately confront the fact that enlargement, which was intended to maintain its diplomatic centrality, actually complicated its relations with key Western partners, and diluted its identity in other regional fora.

These challenges have revealed the limits of ASEAN's post-Cold War success. Originally formed as an experiment in regional cooperation predicated on security concerns, after the Cold War ASEAN placed a new priority on enhancing the quality of its integration, and on 'community'. This raised expectations, both within the Association and outside it, that it could manage regional problems, such as economic crisis and cross-border pollution. It has failed to do so because, despite the illusion of integration, the compact between its members has remained based on loose inter-government cooperation. The culture of avoiding problems, instead of trying to solve them, has persisted. ASEAN's sleight of hand between 'commonality' and 'integration' was exposed most clearly by the economic crisis. But the incorporation of countries like Myanmar, whose authoritarian political system and closed economy represented a new extreme in ASEAN's diversity, would itself have tested the Association's claims to deeper cooperation.

ASEAN's marginal position in the face of the region's economic, political and ecological shocks led to a formal debate over the fundamental tenets of South-east Asian regionalism. Largely as a result of Indonesia's conservative stance, and reluctance among new members to change the rules of the 'club' that they had just joined, the principle of non-interference was confirmed. At the same time, concessions were made to calls for reform from Thailand and the Philippines by mandating 'greater frankness of discussion' on issues with clear cross-border effects. However, 'enhanced interaction' appears to represent merely an uneasy truce. The region's democratic governments must respond to pressure from their societies, and find it difficult to avoid commenting on human-rights issues in other ASEAN states. New members are suspicious of these breaches of the non-interference principle. Attempts to increase the level of 'frankness' incrementally, for example through a regional economic-surveillance mechanism, are proving difficult.

> *ASEAN has been marginalised and divided*

ASEAN has long enjoyed the attention and support of Western capitals, both for its role in South-east Asia and more broadly. In reaffirming its non-interference principle, ASEAN must accept that its claim to manage the South-east Asian order appears much diminished. Outside powers turned to ASEAN to lead the international response to the coup in Cambodia in 1997, forcing the Association to choose between compromising its principle, and damaging its international credibility. Myanmar could pose the same dilemma. Under 'constructive engagement', Yangon allows its ASEAN colleagues to comment privately on its political system, while ASEAN accepts that the West will use the dialogue partnerships to exert pressure on the regime. However, as the breakdown in relations between the EU and ASEAN reveals, this pragmatic accommodation has limits, and would come under severe pressure should Myanmar suffer violent upheaval. This would renew internal criticism from countries keen to change the Association's principles, and would reduce the flexibility which Western countries have shown in dealing with an enlarged ASEAN.

ASEAN's setbacks since July 1997 pose important questions for supporters of an Asia-Pacific community. Both Asia-Pacific institutions, the ARF and APEC, have borrowed elements of ASEAN's approach. While this may indeed be a useful way to build an Asia-Pacific community, ASEAN's problems warn of their limitations. The Association's difficulties, and its preoccupation with specifically South-east Asian concerns, are most likely to damage the ARF given the Association's leading procedural role within it. Neither ASEAN nor Beijing is willing to reduce ASEAN's exclusive responsibility, and the ARF's development may be slow, at least in the medium term.

Consensus within the Association on the benefits of the US regional presence is under pressure, at the same time as Beijing is encouraging ASEAN's experimentation with pan-Asian dialogue. While the Association's support for US engagement has never rested on identical strategic perspectives among its members, the range of views is now greater, and embraces countries with limited, if not negative, relations with Washington. While the economic crisis has confirmed America's indispensability to the region, anti-US sentiment may be a useful political tool for governments struggling with economic adversity. Given this uncertainty, it is crucial that the US reinforces its bilateral relations with key ASEAN countries. Maintaining cooperative relations with Indonesia throughout its transition is the most important task. Beyond this, Vietnam is ASEAN's most influential new member; progress in relations with Hanoi is therefore essential.

Can South-east Asian regionalism have a problem-solving or integrative role? While enlargement has reinforced existing prac- tices, aspirations for a closer community among some of the original members appear to demand a different solution. The culture of non- interference and of avoiding problems is, however, ingrained, and is unlikely to change without a clear signal from the region's leadership. This signal can only really come from Indonesia. The course of the country's transition will therefore be decisive in determining ASEAN's future role.

Indonesia's size and its importance to the Asia-Pacific mean that international organisations and the major powers have an interest in the country's return to political stability and economic growth. At Jakarta's request, international assistance has been forthcoming from a range of sources, including its key bilateral partners in the Consultative Group for Indonesia (CGI), chaired by the World Bank, international financial institutions, primarily the IMF, and the UN. While ASEAN members have played a role, both bilaterally and by contributing to multilateral efforts, ASEAN itself has not, indeed cannot, do so. The depth of international involvement in Indonesia's transition is in marked contrast to ASEAN's purposeful avoidance of entanglement in the country's 'internal affairs'. Should East Timor choose independence, for example, ASEAN would be unlikely to have any more than a nominal role in the potential birth of a nation which could well join its ranks.

Nonetheless, ASEAN does have a role to play whatever the outcome of Indonesia's transition. If the country's political and economic reform goes awry, leaving it stridently nationalistic or struggling to maintain its unity against provincial insurrection, the Association will be forced to confront the possibility of major regional instability. Under these circumstances, ASEAN could be a mechanism for its neighbours to engage the new regime, thereby building confidence. The original members would be galvanised to set aside differences, including those over the Association's operating procedures, and cooperate to engage Indonesia.

ASEAN will be shaken no matter which way Indonesia goes

Should a stable government with reformist convictions emerge in Jakarta, it may contemplate a more open form of inter-action within ASEAN. This would not mean that Indonesia would necessarily demand radical changes. However, a democratic and reformist Indonesia would inevitably approach ASEAN differently. Its readiness to discuss regional issues in a more open way could encourage others to do so. As in the Philippines and Thailand, civil society in Indonesia would press the government over human-rights issues in other South-east Asian states. If an independent East Timor did eventually join ASEAN, it would be likely to challenge the non-interference mantra.

The emergence of a reformist government in Indonesia would renew interest in Thailand and the Philippines in pursuing changes to ASEAN's operating procedures. If post-transition Indonesia favoured a more integrated ASEAN, which would call for some concessions to the Association's insistence on national sovereignty, Malaysia and Singapore would be under pressure to reassess their positions. While ASEAN is unlikely formally to change its treaty commitments, Indonesian leadership could lead to a substantial shift in the Association's operating practices. This would not be without its costs, since it would strain the new members' allegiance to ASEAN, but it may provide the basis for deeper integration between the original members.

Introduction

[1] Goh Chok Tong, Closing Statement, Fifth ASEAN Summit, Bangkok, 15 December 1995, www.aseansec.org.

Chapter 1

[1] All of South-east Asia with the exception of Thailand had been colonised.
[2] 'The Bangkok Declaration, Thailand, 8 August 1967', www.aseansec.org.
[3] Roger Irvine, 'The Formative Years of ASEAN: 1967–1975', in Alison Broinowski (ed.), *Understanding ASEAN* (London: Macmillan, 1982), p. 36.
[4] Michael Leifer, *ASEAN and the Security of South-East Asia* (London: Routledge, 1989), pp. 31–36.
[5] This fear of external support for domestic communist insurgencies was expressed by the Thai delegate to the UN General Assembly in 1965, who defined external foreign intervention as: 'verbal intimidation, infiltration, and subversive activities directed and supported from outside'. See Peter Lyon, *War and Peace in South-East Asia* (London: Oxford University Press, 1969), p. 179.
[6] Dewi Fortuna Anwar, *Indonesia in ASEAN* (Singapore: Institute of South-east Asian Studies (ISEAS), 1994), p. 222.
[7] *Ibid.*, p. 45.
[8] For national views of the Zone of Peace, Freedom and Neutrality (ZOPFAN), see *ibid.*, pp. 180–82.
[9] Tim Huxley, 'ASEAN Security Cooperation', in Alison Broinowski (ed.), *ASEAN into the 1990s* (London: Macmillan, 1990), pp. 89–91.
[10] 'ASEAN and the Question of Cambodia', IISS, *Strategic Comments*, vol. 3, no. 7, September 1997.
[11] Michael Leifer, *The ASEAN Regional Forum*, Adelphi Paper 302 (Oxford: Oxford University Press for the IISS, 1996), p. 6.
[12] Carlyle A. Thayer, 'ASEAN and Indochina: The Dialogue', in Broinowski (ed.), *ASEAN into the*

1990s, p. 139.

[13] Leifer, *The ASEAN Regional Forum*, p. 16.

[14] Goh Chok Tong, quoted in Simon Hay, 'The 1995 ASEAN Summit: Scaling a Higher Peak', *Contemporary South-east Asia*, vol. 18, no. 3, December 1996, p. 256.

[15] Amitav Acharya, 'Sovereignty, Non-intervention and Regionalism', CANCAPS Paper 15 (Toronto: Canadian Consortium for Asia-Pacific Security, 1997), p. 5.

[16] Leifer, *ASEAN and the Security of South-east Asia*, p. 145.

[17] John Ravenhill, 'Economic Cooperation in Southeast Asia', *Asian Survey*, vol. 35, no. 9, September 1995, pp. 854–55.

[18] Chia Siow Yue, 'The ASEAN Free Trade Area', *Pacific Review*, vol. 11, no. 2, 1998, p. 214.

[19] Chin Kin Wah, 'ASEAN in the New Millennium', in Chia Siow Yue and Marcello Pacini (eds), *ASEAN in the New Asia* (Singapore: ISEAS, 1997), p. 148.

[20] Goh Chok Tong, Closing Statement, Fifth ASEAN Summit.

[21] Fidel Ramos, Opening Statement, Fifth ASEAN Summit, Bangkok, 14 December 1995, www.aseansec.org.

[22] Josef Silverstein, 'Constructive Engagement with Burma', paper presented at the conference 'Constructive Engagement in Asia', Bangkok, 20–23 August 1997, p. 23.

[23] Suharto, quoted in Paul Kelly, 'United Region Balances the China Factor', *The Australian*, 30 July 1997, p. 13.

[24] Carlyle A. Thayer, 'Constructive Engagement or Constructive Interference: Reconciling Principles with Effectiveness', paper presented at the conference 'Constructive Engagement in Asia', p. 2.

[25] *Straits Times*, 26 August 1992,

cited in Acharya, 'Sovereignty, Non-intervention and Regionalism', p. 8.

[26] Also in 1996, Papua New Guinea proposed that it should be made a 'permanent associate member' of ASEAN. The country was granted observer status at the ASEAN Ministerial Meeting in 1976, and acceded to the Treaty of Amity and Cooperation after its amendment in 1987 to allow states outside of South-east Asia, with the consent of its signatories, to join. However, these arrangements were not intended to lead to Papua New Guinea becoming an ASEAN member. Port Moresby's permanent associate membership proposal, the terms of which it left vague, received a lukewarm reception from ASEAN members.

[27] Malcolm Chalmers, *Confidence-building in South-East Asia* (Bradford: University of Bradford, 1996), p. 31.

[28] Kusuma Snitwongse, 'ASEAN's Security Cooperation: Searching for a Regional Order', *Pacific Review*, vol. 8, no. 3, 1995, pp. 527–28. On China, see Huxley, 'ASEAN Security Cooperation', in Broinowski (ed.), *ASEAN in the 1990s*, p. 95. The start of very limited defence contact under ASEAN auspices through defence participation in the Senior Officials' Meeting from 1995 did not reflect a substantial change to this position, and neither did the 'golf day' for ASEAN defence ministers held in Indonesia in 1997.

[29] See Leifer, *The ASEAN Regional Forum*, pp. 30–31.

[30] Hadi Soesastro, 'ASEAN and APEC: Do Concentric Circles Work?', *Pacific Review*, vol. 8, no. 3, 1995, p. 476.

[31] 'What Would Confucius Say

Now?', *The Economist*, 25 July 1998, p. 23.
[32] Hanns Maull, Gerald Segal and Jusuf Wanandi (eds), *Europe and the Asia Pacific* (London: Routledge, 1998) p. xi.
[33] Michael Leifer, 'Europe and South-east Asia', in *ibid.*, p. 199.
[34] Warren Christopher, Statement to the US–ASEAN Post-Ministerial Conference (PMC), Bandar Seri Begawan, Brunei, 2–3 August 1995, www.aseansec.org.
[35] Ramos, Opening Statement, Fifth ASEAN Summit.
[36] Mahathir Mohamad, Opening Statement, Fifth ASEAN Summit, www.aseansec.org.

Chapter 2

[1] See, for example, Mahathir, Opening Statement, Fifth ASEAN Summit.
[2] World Bank data, www.worldbank.org.
[3] Leifer, *The ASEAN Regional Forum*, p. 11.
[4] Thayer, 'ASEAN and Indochina', p. 144.
[5] Interviews with officials, Department of Foreign Affairs, Hanoi, 20 April 1998.
[6] Interview with Ministry of Foreign Affairs officials, Jakarta, 27 April 1998.
[7] Interview with Tin Maung Maung Than, Fellow, ISEAS, Singapore, 23 April 1998.
[8] 'Thai PM Warns of Military Strikes against Raiders Crossing Border', *South China Morning Post*, 26 March 1998.
[9] Interview with Singaporean Ambassador-At-Large Tommy Koh, Singapore, 22 April 1998.
[10] See Bertil Lintner, 'Velvet Glove', *Far Eastern Economic Review*, 7 May 1998.
[11] East Asia Analytical Unit, *The New ASEANs* (Canberra: Commonwealth of Australia, 1997), p. 319.
[12] Rodolfo Severino, Asia Policy Lecture, University of Sydney, 22 October 1998, www.aseansec.org.
[13] Mahathir, speech delivered at the opening of the Kuala Lumpur Stock Exchange (KLSE) headquarters, 15 August 1997, quoted in Lim Kok Wing, *Hidden Agenda* (Petaling Jaya: Limkokwing, 1998), p. 25.
[14] 'The Impact of the Crisis on ASEAN Trade', East Asia Economic Summit of the World Economic Forum, Singapore, 13 October 1998.
[15] 'Exports to ASEAN Countries Drop By Over 30 Per Cent', Vietnamese News Agency (VNA), 18 July 1998, in *BBC Summary of World Broadcasts, The Far East* (SWB/FEW) 0548 WB/9, 29 July 1998.
[16] Australian Department of Foreign Affairs and Trade (DFAT), 'Country Brief: Burma (Myanmar)', October 1998, www.dfat.gov.au.
[17] Evelyn Iritani, 'Thai Premier Urges US Patience with Indonesia', *Los Angeles Times*, 16 March 1998, p. 1.
[18] *The Indonesian Fires and Haze of 1997: The Economic Toll* (Singapore: Economy and Environment Program for Southeast Asia, June 1998), p. 3.
[19] Simon Tay, 'What Should Be Done about the Haze', *Indonesian Quarterly*, vol. 26, no. 2, 1998.
[20] Speech by Australian Foreign Minister Alexander Downer, National Press Club, Canberra, 31 March 1999; John Aglionby, 'British Police to Watch Over Timor Ballot', *The Guardian*, p. 17.
[21] Kavi Chongkittavorn, 'Thailand

Can Help', *The Nation*, 8 April 1999.
[22] See, for example, Kavi Chongkittavorn, 'Indonesia To Help Timor into ASEAN', *The Nation*, 17 February 1999; and Amien Rais, speech delivered at the School of Advanced International Studies (SAIS), Washington DC, 9 March 1999.
[23] See, for example, Barry Wain, 'ASEAN Is Facing Its Keenest Challenges To Date', *Asian Wall Street Journal*, 23 February 1998; 'The Limits of Politeness', *The Economist*, 28 February 1998; and Murray Hiebert, 'Out of Its Depth', *Far Eastern Economic Review*, 19 February 1998, p. 26.
[24] Anwar Ibrahim, 'Crisis Prevention', *Newsweek*, 21 July 1997, p. 29.
[25] Acharya, 'Sovereignty, Non-intervention, and Regionalism', p. 12.
[26] *Ibid.*, p. 13.
[27] Surin quoted in Peter Alford, 'Thais Push Radical Shift in ASEAN', *The Australian*, 6 July 1998.
[28] Anwar, 'Crisis Prevention'.
[29] 'Thailand's Non-Paper on the Flexible Engagement Approach', *Press Release 743/2541*, Thai Ministry of Foreign Affairs, 27 July 1998, www.thaiembdc.org.
[30] 'ASEAN Sec-Gen Supports Surin's Intervention Policy', *The Nation*, 30 June 1998.
[31] Domingo Siazon, quoted in Alford, 'Thais Push Radical Shift'.
[32] For a Singaporean perspective on ASEAN reform, see Tommy Koh, 'East Asians Should Learn from Western Europe', *International Herald Tribune*, 10 July 1998.
[33] Hun Sen, quoted in Kao Kim Hourn and Jeffrey A. Kaplan (eds), *Cambodia's Future in ASEAN: Dynamo or Dynamite* (Phnom Penh: Cambodian Institute for Cooperation and Peace, 1998).
[34] Severino, Asia Policy Lecture.
[35] *Ibid.*
[36] 'Burma Hits Back at Moves to "Interfere"', *South China Morning Post*, 28 July 1998.
[37] 'Myanmar Can Expect No Let Up to Thai Fire', *The Nation*, 29 July 1998.
[38] Ian Stewart, 'Malaysia Delivers Jolt to ASEAN Ties', *South China Morning Post*, 21 October 1998.
[39] Goh Chok Tong, speech to the Asia Society, Sydney, 2 March 1999.
[40] 'ASEAN Vision 2020', www.aseansec.org.

Chapter 3

[1] Qian Qichen, Opening Statement, ASEAN–China PMC, 28 July 1997, www.aseansec.org.
[2] See Allen S. Whiting, 'ASEAN Eyes China: The Security Dimension', *Asian Survey*, vol. 37, no. 4, April 1997, pp. 299–322.
[3] ASEAN's Declaration on the South China Sea does not define the extent of 'the South China Sea', although geographically the term covers the Paracel Islands and the Gulf of Tonkin. See Mark J. Valencia, *China and the South China Sea Disputes*, Adelphi Paper 298 (Oxford: Oxford University Press for the IISS, 1995), p. 34.
[4] See Michael Leifer, *China in Southeast Asia: Independence and Accommodation*, CAPS Paper 14 (Taipei: Chinese Council of Advanced Policy Studies (CAPS), 1997), p. 5.
[5] 'ASEAN–China Summit Declaration', 16 December 1997, www.aseansec.org.
[6] Severino, quoted in Rigoberto Tiglao, ''Tis the Season', *Far Eastern*

Economic Review, 24 December 1998.

[7] Michael Richardson, 'Japan's Lack of Leadership Pushes ASEAN toward Cooperation with China', *International Herald Tribune*, 17 April 1998; 'China Voices Concern for Chinese Indonesians', *Straits Times*, 16 July 1998.

[8] See, for example, 'Japan Makes Aid-for-Support Offer to Asia', *Straits Times*, 13 November 1998; and 'To Japan's Credit', *ibid.*, 24 December 1998.

[9] China was represented by the Vice-President Hu Jintao, rather than the President, Jiang Zemin, as had been the case at the 1997 ASEAN summit which celebrated the Association's thirtieth anniversary.

[10] Qian, 'Opening Statement'.

[11] Speech by Secretary of State Madeleine Albright, Pacific Council and the Los Angeles World Affairs Council, Los Angeles, 23 July 1997.

[12] Interviews with US administration officials, Washington DC, April 1998.

[13] 'Chairman's Statement', ASEAN PMC, Senior Officials' Meeting, Singapore, 20–21 May 1993, cited in Leifer, *The ASEAN Regional Forum*, p. 20.

[14] Ali Alatas, statement opening the US–ASEAN dialogue session, Subang Jaya, Malaysia, 28 July 1998, www.aseansec.org.

[15] 'East Asia's Delicate Balance', *The Economist*, 25 July 1998, p. 20.

[16] 'KL Renews Call to Form East Asian Grouping', *Straits Times Interactive*, 22 August 1998, www.straitstimes.asia1.com.

[17] Akiko Kato, 'Japan Responsible for Sparking Growth in Asia', *Mainichi Daily News*, 13 January 1999, p. 2.

[18] Al Gore, Remarks at the APEC Business Summit, Kuala Lumpur, 16 November 1998, www.whitehouse.gov.

[19] Mahathir, quoted in Lim Kok Wing, *Hidden Agenda*, p. 97.

[20] Mari Pangestu, 'Give Us Some Credit, Please', *Time Asia*, 1 June 1998, p. 29.

[21] Leifer, *The ASEAN Regional Forum*, p. 27.

[22] Jose T. Almonte, 'Ensuring Security the "ASEAN Way"', *Survival*, vol. 30, no. 4, Winter 1997–98, p. 81.

[23] The Joint Cooperation Committee deals with trade and investment issues under the European Union (EU)'s 'Pillar One', involving legally binding agreements between the European Community and its partners. Discussions of issues beyond trade are classified as 'Pillar Two'.